The
Rich Is Better
W O R K B O O K

The **Rich Is Better** WORKBOOK

Judy Resnick

Golden Books

New York

Golden Books®

888 Seventh Avenue
New York, NY 10106

Designed by Meryl Sussman Levavi, digitext, inc.

Manufactured in the United States of America

10 9 8 7 6 5 4 3 2 1

CONTENTS

1

MY STORY

My name is Judy Resnick, and I'm chairman of the Resnick Group, a money-management company based in Los Angeles. I've written this workbook so that you can learn about the various aspects of taking care of your money, then sit down and fill out some financial forms that will prepare you to do just that. You can complete them using your records, or with the assistance of a friend, your husband or partner, or an accountant. Whatever process you choose, when you're finished with this workbook, you'll have a realistic grasp of how much you have, how much you want, and what you can expect from your financial future.

Please don't be intimidated by the thought of tackling these issues. The material in this book is easy to understand and the forms are simple to complete. And when you're done, I believe you'll feel better about your finances than you ever thought possible. You see, once you've filled out all the relevant forms, you'll have one very important thing you didn't have before, and that is knowledge.

Yes, knowledge. It may be the most important part of any intelligent financial plan. How can you plan for your future if you don't know how much you have in the present? You need a solid perception of who you are financially—how much you earn, how much you spend, how much you have on hand, and how much you can expect to have in the future.

So take the time to read the information and fill out the forms in this book. Maybe you'll learn that you're better off than you thought. Maybe you'll even get into the habit of filling out these kinds of forms regularly, which is the smartest thing you can do.

Even if you learn that your situation is worse than you'd expected, just having gained that knowledge means you'll be a little better off. For once you know, you'll be able to do something about it.

And that's what I most want to say to you: Do something about it!

The reason I feel qualified to write this book is that, more than likely, I've *been* you at some point. The circumstances of my life have provided experiences so diverse that I've had to play numerous and varied roles. I have been a young girl in a family where only men were supposed to work; a newlywed in a male-dominated relationship; a married woman without a career; a divorced woman without a career; a single mother raising two children; a would-be heiress who discovered that her millionaire father had gambled away all his money; a broke, unemployed job-seeker; a successful wage earner at a major stock brokerage; and an entrepreneur running her own company. And that's just a part of my story.

Sure, there are still many of you whom I haven't been—and never will be. But the bottom line is: I'm not just a "suit." I'm not some gal who, after a thorough education in finance, was groomed from the age of 21 to sell investment vehicles to the rich and famous. I'm not even someone who was brought up to know anything at all about money.

The truth is, like many women (especially those around my age, 57), I was sheltered and supported throughout most of my life. My father protected me from everyone and everything. In fact, I used to joke that I was so independent I didn't have to answer to anyone—except, of course, to Daddy.

If you've read my first book, *I've Been Rich, I've Been Poor, Rich Is Better,* you already know the story. If not, here it is in a nutshell:

The first part of my life couldn't have been more mundane. I was born in 1941, just before the attack on Pearl Harbor. My father, Lou, worked hard for a living, selling refrigerators. (Later he moved on to higher-paying occupations, such as owning bowling alleys.) Fran, my mother, stayed home, like a good 1950s mother should. Fran took care of the household and Lou took care of the money. That's the way they thought it should be, so that's the way it was.

I grew up in New Jersey with my two siblings. The only shock in my life up to that point occurred when one day we picked up and moved from the East Coast to the West—along with several million other families. So I became a California girl, which, as in the Beach Boys songs, meant bikinis, convertibles, and fun in the sun.

I did have a few illnesses as a child. One cost me an ovary, and another was so serious I was housebound for an entire year. But other than that, the Resnicks were 98.6 degrees normal.

Being normal meant my parents trained my brother to work for a living and understand the value of money. I, on the other hand, was trained to stay thin, look good, and find a man. When my mother talked about my future, she wanted the best for me. And what she meant by that was, the best husband. Someone to watch over me. And the best career? As they say in New Jersey, fuhgeddaboutit. It was all about catching the man who could support you, not finding the career that would let you support yourself.

My parents did allow me to attend college for a while, but I quickly lost interest in my studies. All I wanted to do was date cute boys and have fun, knowing that some day one of them would turn out to be my knight in shining armor.

When one of those cute boys, Martin, proposed to be my knight, I consented.

Now I was a married woman, and for all I knew, this was my life's destiny. Didn't Mother always say to marry well, with the implied message being, *stay* married?

But I couldn't stay married to Martin. He was no knight. The poor guy. His armor was rusted, his shield was cracked. After a wretched, vile marriage, I had had enough. We then went through an ugly, contentious divorce that left me with nothing—except the two most wonderful gifts of my lifetime: my daughters, Audrey and Stacey. They are today, as always, my pride, my love, my joy.

At the age of 26, I was alone again. So I did what any California girl would do in the mid-1960s. I had fun. I experimented with drugs. I dated more guys. I lived the high life.

But the high life wasn't as high as I'd hoped, and after a life-threatening bout with cancer and a serious drug-abuse problem, I ended up institutionalizing myself. That wasn't much fun either, but at least it ended my drug problem. The cancer, too, was cured.

I came out of that hospital ready to face the world with strength and confidence. Of course, I was still relying on my dad to pay for everything. I moved into a lovely little house in Beverly Hills purchased with a loan from my father, hired a live-in house-keeper, and, while the kids were in school, I played tennis. I acted as though I had no responsibilities in the world, because, in reality, I took no *financial* responsibility whatsoever.

But all good things—and most bad things, too—come to an end. One summer day in 1976 my father left the house, flew to Las Vegas with my mother, and dropped dead of a brain embolism.

After we recovered from the shock, we were at least consoled by the thought that we had inherited a fortune. Dad was rich, wasn't he? He'd certainly lived as though he was. There had always been money for anything we wanted.

But no-oooo. We received almost nothing. It seemed that Dad had suffered from a gambling problem, and instead of several million dollars, we inherited dozens of markers from Las Vegas casinos. (One called to ask for its money. "We're broke," we said. "You already have everything.")

Suddenly being a coddled little girl was no longer an option. Still, I did have a house, and some income that my father had given me prior to his death, through his business partners.

But before I could settle into my new life, both my mother and sister were killed in a plane crash. Again, I collapsed into grief. And before I could adjust to this new loss, Dad's ex-partners informed me that they were buying out the one piece of income I had, leaving me with only enough money to live for another few years.

Then, a few months later, I found myself back in the hospital, this time with an unidentifiable affliction that the doctors told me might necessitate amputating an arm, or worse. And they'd found a tumor on my one remaining ovary, and would have to perform a hysterectomy—assuming, of course, that I made it through the other operation.

So there I was, lying on a hospital gurney in tears as the doctors prepared to cart away my body parts. Who had time to be spoiled anymore? It was time to grow up. And even though I was now over 40, with two daughters and no education, no career, and no job experience, I couldn't afford to feel sorry for myself.

Now, I'm not telling you these things to upset you. I'm telling you because bad things happen to regular people like you and me. It's not just in the newspapers. It's real life. Face it as a mature adult, and you'll get mature results.

And for once I did respond as an adult. For the first time, I realized that only I was responsible for my own life. For the first time I felt real courage, stamina, and endurance. I had to live—for my children's sake, and for my own.

With my renewed strength I looked the surgeon in the eyes and told him that if I died in this operation, I'd be leaving behind two orphans, so he'd better make it work. He did.

After the operation I returned to therapy to deal with losing my family. Only, once I had grieved enough, it was time to *do* something.

But what? "You need a j-o-b," a smart friend told me, and after I looked up the word in the dictionary and fainted, I realized that he was right. But I had no skills. Who was going to hire a middle-aged woman who'd spent her life hiding from responsibility? I had nothing to offer anyone. I sat on the beach and cried and cried.

But crying only lasts so long, and there was no way I was going to see my darling daughters suffer. So I gathered all my strength and decided to get a real job once and for all.

I didn't even know what kind of job to look for, but in the meantime I'd received a $50,000 settlement from the airline on whose flight my mother and sister had been killed and had turned it over to a stockbroker. In a strange way, I was hoping he'd lose it all, since it felt like such dirty money to me.

I got my wish. The man indeed lost every cent. His idea of smart investing wasn't to buy a few solid stocks and stay with them. Instead, he played the markets, gambling and rolling dice.

He did, however, make a nice commission for himself.

Well, I thought, why shouldn't *I* be a stockbroker, too? I'm as smart as this man, and maybe I can even make money for my clients.

Somehow it sounded right, so I went out and bought all the books I could find on how to be a broker and read each one. I sold my house to give me enough cash to live. Then I purchased a nice white linen suit—my entire wardrobe at the time was tennis outfits and sneakers—and I interviewed for jobs.

This turned out to be the toughest task of my life. But one day, after being turned down over and over for being undereducated, or for lacking experience, I got a break: Drexel Burnham Lambert offered me a position in their training program.

In 1982, at the age of 41, I had a real job! I was a stockbroker. Now, at the time I couldn't tell a municipal bond from a bail bond. And I knew nothing about savings, nothing about finance, nothing about stocks. All I knew about money was how to spend it.

The position required six months' training, after which each trainee had to pass a test. I geared up for that test as I had for nothing else in my life, studying and studying until the test day came. I was so ready that I aced it.

That first year I continued to work sixteen hours a day, trying to understand as much as I could. While concentrating on research, I became caught up in high-yield bonds, in which Drexel specialized. Soon I was doing well—I still remember how much money I made my first year: $106,000!

And I continued to do well—so much so that by 1987, I'd decided I didn't want to be a retail stockbroker anymore. So I approached the boss's boss, Mike Milken, with an idea. Milken was the most famous person at Drexel, but I didn't know him at all. Yet he gave me twenty minutes to make my pitch, which he loved. Suddenly I was selling to smaller institutions, people the big guys at Drexel didn't have time for.

Now I found out the true purpose of capital. This was my biggest lesson in financial reality. You know all those rich guys you always hear about for no other reason than that they're rich—the ones raising $250 million for this deal, $500 million for that? Well, the reason they were getting even richer was because they had capital, which meant that they had money to invest in the equity of different companies.

I decided that it was time for women to become part of that group. And I realized that to do so, you and I would have to save our money. That's how we would get our capital. No one was raising money for us, so we would take what we had and invest it in the marketplace.

I learned being financially smart isn't about getting rich. It's about having enough money to be able to make money off your money.

In 1988, I left Drexel to start my own firm, because I had also learned that ownership is key to wealth. Ownership is also a risk, but it was one I was now prepared to take, professionally and personally. Finally I knew I was good at something, and I wanted to take advantage of that.

Oh, yes, fate intervened in my life several more times: There was the fire that burned up all my possessions, and several other crises. Above all, there was the extraordinary discovery that, nevertheless, I could lead my life without a man. I could lead it with a man, too, but I'd finally realized that when the chips were down, I, and no one else, was responsible for myself.

The idea that a woman could exist in this world without a man, and exist happily, had always struck me as exotic. I knew that other women had done it, but I never believed they could be truly happy—even less that they were safe. What if a financial disaster came along? Who would take care of them then?

But enough calamities had come along in my own life to make me realize that I was a survivor, with or without anyone else. At the end of the day, it was all up to me.

This isn't to say that I don't think men can be great. I do, very much so. It's just that I've made the wonderful transition from needing men to liking them.

You can read more about my experiences in my first book. Now it's time to pay attention to *you,* and find out what kind of financial health you're enjoying.

2

QUIZ: ARE YOU READY TO TAKE CARE OF YOUR MONEY?

Like it or not—and I, for one, like it—there are inherent differences between the male and female of the species. Volumes have been written on all of them; for starters, let's talk about how women tend to be more nurturing than men. Even today, despite the enormous strides women have made in the workplace, in government, and in society at large, tests show that if you present a boy and a girl with a choice of toys, the majority of boys will reach for the guns, the soldiers, and the tools, while the girls reach for dolls they can hold, nurture, and nourish.

So why can't we hold, nurture, and nourish our money? Why do we run into so many psychological stumbling blocks that stop us from becoming as financially astute as males?

No one really knows the reason. Still, I suggest that much of the problem has to do with our relatively recent entry into the let's-take-care-of-our-money sweepstakes. Men have ruled this domain for centuries; women are neophytes.

But that's no reason to fail. It simply means we have to pay more attention to what we're doing to get it right. And we will— once we overcome certain psychological demons that still jump out and attack us when we're not looking, as shown in the following box.

WHY WOMEN FAIL TO ACHIEVE THEIR GOALS

Accompanied by actual remarks women have written down on seminar forms, or have volunteered in meetings.

PARENTAL INFLUENCE (My dad told me I couldn't make it on my own, and Father knows best.)

FAILURE TO ESTABLISH A GOAL (I'd rather buy a dress now than save later.)

IGNORANCE (You mean I have to take care of my own money?)

BAD TRACK RECORD (But I lost money the last time I invested it. I don't want to try again.)

DEBT (It doesn't matter if I've maxed out on this credit card. I have another one.)

PREVIOUS BAD ADVICE (But that man told me I couldn't lose if I invested in the Asian markets.)

INFLATION (I put all my money in an account that earned me 4 percent. Wasn't that enough?)

TAXES (So I spend everything I make. I mean, I don't spend <u>more</u> than I make. How was I to know I was supposed to pay taxes before I got to spend it?)

PROCRASTINATION (Oh, for goodness sake, I'll get it together. Just give me another year.)

LACK OF SELF-CONFIDENCE (There's no way I can take care of my own money.)

LACK OF GOALS (Look, I make a good salary today, and I'm still young. I don't think I need to worry about retirement yet.)

FEAR OF MONEY (I like making money, and I like spending money. I'm just terrified of dealing with it.)

FEAR OF BEING INDEPENDENT (I'll never get married if I seem too powerful.)

PLEASURE IN BEING DEPENDENT (I think it's great that you can take care of yourself, but me, well, I don't have to worry...my husband would never leave me [told to me by a woman who was divorced a year later].)

FEAR OF SUCCESS (I'm just not a successful person—it's not who I am, and it's not who I'm ever going to be.)

FEAR OF TRUST (I'd like to have a money manager. I just don't feel good about letting anyone else handle my affairs.)

SUPERSTITION (I know if I put my money in the stock market now, it'll go right down. That's just the way my luck always goes.)

PLAIN STUPIDITY (Who gives a damn whether I have money tomorrow? I'm happy today.)

The following test is designed to help you locate some of these obstacles within yourself. You'll be asked to read some scenarios borrowed from my clients' histories (completely disguised, of course), then figure out what you would do if you were in that woman's situation.

Now, don't get nervous. There are no absolute right or wrong answers here. Even within each question there's room for appeal. Maybe you won't agree with some of my psychological views. Maybe you've made a fortune while completely disobeying one of my rules, and that's fine. Congratulations. I hope you'll write a book, too.

But there *is* general agreement on what makes a good investor, and what doesn't. All I'm trying to do here is help you identify some of the traits of a person who's good with money, and those of a person who isn't.

Most important, please be honest. Even if you know that your preferred answer is wrong, if it reflects who you really are, go with it. You won't learn anything if you're not honest with yourself. That's one truism that applies to everyone, everywhere, every time.

1. You're a single woman who's been working for a decade as an advertising executive, and for the most part things have gone well. Last month, however, your company lost its biggest account, and they let go ten senior associates, including you. Still, you know you're readily employable, so even though nothing's on the horizon right now, you're confident that some great offers will come your way soon. In the meantime, you have enough savings to get you through an entire year.

Today you were at a new store in your favorite shopping center and you saw a handbag you love. It cost $700, which is much more than you've ever spent on a bag. But this one's fabulous.

Do you:

1. Buy it. The bag is you. You have confidence in yourself. A new job is bound to come along.
2. Buy two—you have a tendency to lose the things you like the most—then go off and have a few drinks to celebrate.
3. Hold off until you have a job, even if it means carrying that old worn-out leather bag for another few months.

If you jumped right at (1), you may well be a spendaholic. Be careful. Having confidence in yourself is one thing; having a job is another.

Spendaholism can be a serious impediment to developing financial smarts. There's often no stopping it. The spendthrifts I've met have a tendency to go way beyond their means. Spendaholism is not unlike other "isms," such as alcoholism. Sufferers delude themselves, pretending they don't really *have* to spend money—but they do. And once they start, spendaholics can't stop. Then they end up so overburdened with credit-card debt, bankruptcy looms just around the corner.

The worst part of spendaholism: It can destroy more than just your pocketbook. Like anything done to excess, it's pernicious and dangerous—in fact, I've seen spendaholism ruin many marriages. As Aristotle said, everything in moderation.

Often hand in hand with spendaholism is self-destruction, such as buying two bags and going on a bender for the hell of it, as in (2). And yes, I've seen people do this, and much worse. The problem is, most of those who'd go with this choice wouldn't admit it. If you can admit it, you're on the road to recovery.

As you know, self-destruction can take many forms, such as heavy alcohol use, hurting those around you, or simply refusing to do what's best for your life. Being self-destructive with money means spending it in noxious ways. It means taking your money—hard-earned or inherited, it doesn't matter—and throwing it away on drugs, cars, or other things without real value. I've run into too many people for whom the abuse of money became part of the general abuse of their lives. There was the famous actor who spent everything he had on cocaine. Another celebrity bought houses, wrecked them, sold them at a loss, and couldn't have cared less until he went broke. Then there was the dishonest stockbroker who dipped into his clients' accounts to support his extravagant lifestyle; when he got caught, he shot himself. These people can't build for their future, because in order to build a good future, you have to want a good future. Please: Make a happy, responsible future your primary financial goal.

So, yes, just as you thought, (3) is the best answer.

2. You've been avoiding the stock market for years, although you've been doing well at work, receiving regular raises, and living more or less within your budget. Your ex-husband, with whom you're still friendly, contributes his fair share to your kids' education, and you have relatively little to worry about financially.

The other day you looked at your bank account and saw that you have more than $250,000 in savings. Meanwhile, the stock market has been rising and rising. You know you need to invest your money, or inflation will eat it all up. But everyone you know keeps saying that the market can't rise any further.

As you keep hearing these dire predictions, you look at your money so safe and sound in the bank, and you wonder what, if anything, to do.

Do you:

1. Decide to wait a while until the market inevitably corrects itself.
2. Go ahead and invest anyway.
3. Ask your astrologer for her advice.

If you picked (1), we have to talk. In my experience there are two kinds of people who take that route.

The first group I call the Perfect Timers. These are the people who think that they can time the market exactly right. Oh, they say, I can't get into the market now—it's too late, it's too early, everyone says wait a bit, everyone says it's going to crash.

Well, how often is everyone right? Very rarely. In 1996 one of my closest and wisest friends advised me to sell all my stocks, because he knew for certain that the market was about to dive. Everyone who was anyone, he confided, was selling. Luckily I didn't take his advice, for if I had, my net worth would be much less than it is today.

Yes, you should pay attention to the outside world. Yes, the markets do affect you. But if you wait and wait and wait to invest, you'll never start. Maybe you will have some bad luck, and after you invest your hard-earned money, your stocks will fall. But historically, stocks have always come back, in spades. So invest when the time is right for you, not when everyone else says the time is right. Sorry to say, there's no such thing as perfect timing. There is, however, good research, solid advice, and the need to put your money somewhere other than in a bank.

The second group of women who pick (1) are what I call the Friday the Thirteenthers. These are the women who are convinced that breaking a mirror means seven years' bad luck, and that walking under a ladder is going to land them in the hospital, and who also say, "I just know if I put my money in the stock market, it's going to crash." Right. The whole world economy depends on what you do with your money. Think about it. Are you really the most powerful person in the universe? No, you're not. Get over it. Neither your karma nor your money is going to drive the market down (or up).

This group is also prone to try (3). Not that I have anything against astrology (I'm a Sagittarius myself)—or anything else that helps get you through the day. But there's a place for everything, and I have yet to be convinced that because you're a Libra, you should hold back on investing until the planets are more favorable, or that because you're a Scorpio, your portfolio should have a heavy emphasis on bonds.

The best answer here is the one you probably thought was most obvious: (2). When you have the money to invest for your future, do it without delay. In the long run, you'll be glad you did.

3.

You're in a solid marriage and you have two terrific young kids. Both you and your husband work: He's an artist, you're a partner in a law firm. Although your husband is doing well, it's your income that takes care of the family.

Neither of you has a particularly good track record when it comes to savings, and your IRA isn't enough to support you for more than a month. On the other hand, you have no outstanding debts, and you've been good about paying off your credit cards; as a result, you have a great credit rating.

Recently your firm received a huge bonus, and you shared in this windfall to the tune of $50,000. You're not exactly sure what to do with the money, but your husband says to act in whatever way you feel is best.

Do you:

1. Go out and spend it on a great new car. You deserve it.
2. Place it in the bank where it's nice and safe, because it's your only savings.
3. Talk to your best friend, who says her broker is a genius. When you call him, he tells you about his new idea for selling short, which he says will double your money. You go for it.

If you picked (1), go back and look at the first question. You don't have the savings to do this, good credit notwithstanding. Weren't you paying attention?

Many women are indeed afraid of risks, and they always seem to feel comfortable with (2). But many of these women have already taken a much larger risk, namely marrying a man and then depending on him and him alone to take care of their money. This is a huge risk, and one that makes no sense in the 1990s. Even if hubby turns out to be a wonderful man, that doesn't mean he's a wonderful money manager. And even if he turns out to be wonderful with money, that doesn't mean that he won't want to keep most of his wealth if you end up in an unhappy divorce.

It's not unnatural to be afraid of risk—that's just part of life. And sometimes you should be afraid. Many risks are indeed crazy. I would never tell you to parachute out of a plane or bungee jump off a bridge unless you were completely sure of yourself and your instructor—and unless you took out a great insurance policy as well.

But investing in the stock market is not the same as taking crazy risks. Is it a major risk to invest your money in a venerable company with a documented history of good returns? Is it a major risk to ask the research department of a major stock brokerage house for its best recommendations? No, it's not.

If you picked (3) you're not afraid of crazy risk, but you should be. Taking crazy risks is a dangerous as taking no risks. When you're afraid to risk your money, it slowly dissipates due to inflation; when you take wild risks, your money is likely to disappear even more quickly. Yes, you may make a fortune. But if you're going to put your faith in chance, you might as well buy a lottery ticket, because a lottery ticket's a lot cheaper.

There are extremes on either side. I knew a woman who got a divorce settlement for $750,000 in the form of a check, and she was too afraid even to cash it. She held on to it for four months. Then she finally put it in a CD, and was still afraid to touch it. How did I meet her? Her psychiatrist sent her to me—he felt she needed more than just emotional counseling, or she wouldn't have any money left. (He was probably afraid she wouldn't be able to pay his bills.)

So the correct answer here was none of the above. Yes, I know it wasn't listed. But sometimes the answer to a financial problem isn't staring you in the face. Learn to resist bad ideas and influences, and wait for what you know is right.

4. You're a young, ambitious woman from an upper-middle-class family with a good job in the entertainment industry. You're very detail-oriented, which your bosses love—nothing seems to get past you. You're financially astute, you save your company money on every big project, and you know where every penny is being spent.

You enjoy your job, but someday you want to go off on your own so that you can be your own boss.

In the meantime, you're leading the life of a young executive: driving an expensive car, eating well, wearing nice clothes. But since you have a long-term goal, you also know that you must save, so you decide to work with a certified financial planner (CFP). Every time you look at your bank account you're surprised to see how little money is in it. You know that someone smart can find out where you're going wrong.

The CFP is indeed smart. She tells you that you're spending more than $5000 a month and, at that rate, you'll soon be in debt.

You know this figure is ridiculous, because you track every penny.

Do you:

1. Leave. Since you know money well, it's obvious this CFP doesn't know what she's talking about. You'd be better off elsewhere.
2. Admit that you might be wrong.
3. Tell her that you don't have to worry because your folks have money, and some day you and your siblings will inherit that.

One of the biggest roadblocks I run into concerning money is denial. I didn't spend it (except maybe I did). I keep to a budget (except on special occasions). I never take vacations (except the ones to Europe). And on and on.

Even women who are excellent at their jobs, superb at running the household, and in every other way completely capable can be out of touch when it comes to how much they have, how much they spend, and how much they save.

But here, as in any other part of your life, the results of denial wait for you, lurking in the dark corners, springing at you when you least expect it. Because no matter how much you lie to yourself, the truth always comes out someday. There's no getting around it: Pretending you don't spend money isn't the same thing as *not* spending money. Your creditors aren't interested in your daydreams. They just want your cash.

This is why (1) is so dangerous.

I have several friends who've chosen to live in denial. One of them, Brenda, brags continually about her savings; having that makes her feel like a responsible person. Meanwhile, she owes tens of thousands of dollars on several credit cards, but she doesn't consider that debt. Oh, she says, I could pay that off whenever I want to. But she doesn't. So Brenda really doesn't have any savings at all. On top of that, she's paying 18 percent interest on her debt, which just keeps growing larger and larger. Trust me. Reality, not diamonds, is a girl's best friend.

As far as I'm concerned, denial and living in fantasy are the same thing. Both signify that you're out of touch with real life, which means that you don't really know what's going on, which means that no one's watching your money closely. Picking (3) signals trouble. So many women tell me that their parents are wealthy, or that their husbands earn a great living, or that they've never had to worry about money because somehow it always seems to fall in their laps. Right? Wrong.

For instance, maybe your parents do have some money but for how long? Maybe they'll want to spend it on themselves. Maybe their medical expenses will eat it up. Maybe you and your siblings will fight over it. Maybe the government will take out so much due to your folks poor estate planning that there's not much left. Don't count your chickens before they're taxed.

I love to fantasize, too, but I don't let it control me. Save fantasy for the nighttime. During the day, you need to take stock of things and know the truth. That's why (2) is the right answer—not just here, but often elsewhere in life, too.

---

5. You're a former teacher whose husband, Albert, died last year at age 66, which is a few years older than you are. Al left you in fairly good financial shape, which is lucky for you, since while you were married you seldom paid much attention to money. Al always said that he could handle the finances as long as you took care of the domestic side of things. So he did, and you did, and now he's gone.

You have some income from a bond portfolio Al set up a few years ago, a pension from your teaching career, and, in a few years, social security. But you need to supplement all that with income from the $500,000 you've discovered in Al's bank accounts, so you can continue to live in the style you enjoyed when Al was alive.

Your idea is to find a broker (Al's longtime broker has retired to the South Seas). So you ask a friend for a name, and you give the broker she recommends a visit. This woman seems somewhat harsh and rushed, but she tells you not to worry because she'll take care of everything.

In response:

1. You are so glad the woman sounds like Al that you agree to everything.

2. You take an immediate dislike to the woman and get up and leave.
3. You don't like the woman much, but you think you ought to go with her anyway.

Maybe you won't admit it, or maybe you'd like to pretend that (1) isn't who you really are, but too many women decide that someone else should be taking care of their money—it doesn't have to be a man.

Why do women so often do this? Think back to the box on page 9—sometimes it's because they're afraid to take control of their financial lives; sometimes it's because they consider money too baffling; and sometimes it's due to fear of failure. In this last case, if your money goes south, you can always blame the person you hired instead of yourself. But really, if you're complaining that she bought all these bad stocks, where were you when she bought them? I run into Bawling Blamers all the time, women who yell about how others hurt them. Funny how it's never their own fault.

Choosing (1) is also a sign of being overly dependent, which is an issue you might want to discuss with a therapist. Likewise (3) is another sign of this problem. If you are given to this way of dealing with money, be forewarned. Passivity isn't the answer. Sticking your head in the sand doesn't mean the world has disappeared. It just means you can't see it. The world, however, can still see you, all vulnerable with your butt stuck up in the air. Is that how you wish others to perceive you?

If you chose (2), good. Even though you know nothing about finance, you still know enough to trust your own instincts. Now, if this scenario occurs with everyone you meet, you may be paranoid. Or, as in situation number 4, if it's simply that you don't want to hear the truth, then you're in denial.

But you don't have to work with the first person you meet. If you don't like her, walk. Find someone else. Your gut may be the smartest part of your body. Trust it. I never started making money until I began trusting my own instincts. I still do. When my gut says walk, I walk; when it says buy, I buy.

So if you're interviewing people to handle your money, and you hear alarm bells, whether it's because of a person's words, body language, or some other ineffable feeling, trust your gut.

6. You're a single woman in your forties who's doing very well financially. You've been so busy at work that you've barely paid attention to your finances. But now your mother, with whom you've had a terrible relationship, has died, leaving you half a million dollars—money she inherited from your father and then put into a bank account while living frugally off her social security and pension. In fact, given her lifestyle, you had no idea that money was even there. Why didn't she ever spend it, you wonder?

You find a money manager whom you like, and since you have some time to go before you retire, he recommends that you put your money into a growth portfolio. He warns you not to worry if you see some dips over the years. There'll be rises, too, he promises. That's the way it is.

When he asks you for permission to go ahead, you:

1. Tell him that your mother ended up with that much money only by keeping it in the bank, and you'd like to do the same.
2. Tell him that you don't care about money—there are more important values. You'd rather give it to charity or spend it on clothes. You didn't get along with your mother anyway.
3. Agree.

So you think this one is easy? Maybe it seems obvious to you that (3) is the best choice. But then why do so few women I know actually pick it?

Too many women are locked into their family's history. If their fathers had Depression mentalities, they do, too. So they're afraid to spend, to invest, to take care of themselves. If their mothers were convinced that only banks were safe, they are, too; and they fear any investment that isn't insured.

The problem here is that the Depression is over, and it's time to face reality. You can't afford to let your family's preconceptions dictate your life today. Just as you might consult a counselor to deal with other issues arising from your childhood, you might want to consider how many of your financial habits today are actually adopted from your parents', and no longer make sense. Don't repeat history, particularly if it wasn't great to begin with. Instead, create a better history.

And who do so many women read (2) and think, I'd never act like that, and then do so anyway? I've run into dozens of people who don't believe that they deserve to make, or have, money. Now, these are people who really need counseling. I've met or heard of so many who had it all, and then threw it away because they were convinced that somehow having money wasn't right, or it didn't reflect who they really were, or that someone else deserved it more.

But the truth is, it's part of you, so accept it and own it. Charity is wonderful, but it begins at home; you can't grow someone else's garden if you can't grow you own.

Now, if you did something bad to get that money, maybe you should feel guilty. But the sad thing is that crooks seldom feel bad. It's usually those who have no reason to feel guilt who feel it the most.

By choosing (3), you understand that patience is indeed a virtue. And it's one of the most important character traits necessary for being smart with your dollars.

Investing isn't about instant gratification. This is a long-term process, and there's no way to rush it. Instead, you slowly add to your capital through your savings; you make sure your investments make sense; you don't check the paper every day; and if your stock falls, you don't sell. This isn't shooting craps, waiting for the results of one roll of the dice. The worst thing that can happen to a person who likes to gamble is for him to go to Las Vegas and win the first time. He thinks that's the way it always happens. It doesn't. Likewise, if you're not knowledgeable, the worst that can happen to your first stock purchase is that it immediately goes up twenty points. Now you think that's the way it's supposed to be, and you want everything else to behave similarly. It won't. Trust solid market research and be patient. Think of gardening, where you plant seeds now and reap the fruits later. If investing is a game at all, it's a waiting game.

7. You're a young career woman with enough money to start investing a little of it. Good for you. Now you're faced with all the options that can accompany investment.

You aren't working with a money manager; instead you've

decided to hire a broker. You listen to her tips, consult with friends, read the papers, and work hard to make your stock and bond selections.

As your portfolio rises with the bull market, you have more and more to invest. And you're looking at new sources. Today you got a call from your sister's best friend, who works at the Huge Fortune 500 Company; she's convinced that her company is about to merge with the Even Bigger 500 Company, which means that its shares will skyrocket. Meanwhile, you see that this stock has been trading heavily—it does indeed look as though people are buying.

Do you:

1. Buy many shares of the Huge Fortune 500 Company because as far as you know, your sister's best friend is the closest thing you'll ever get to a well-placed source.
2. Look into the situation, and see if everyone else is buying. If they are, then you buy, too.
3. Call up a friend of yours who happens to be on the company's board of directors and get an inside tip.

If you chose (1), you suffer from what I call Black Line Fever. Don't invest in the rumor mill. Just because the telephone is alive with scuttlebutt doesn't mean it's true. Buying on the basis of a well-done research report is one thing, but if you tell me the West Coast is buying the East Coast, I'll tell *you* I have a bridge to sell you. Too many people have lost too much money to rumors and slick salesmen guaranteeing get-rich-quick money. One of my oldest friends fell prey to a woman who called with a promise of a 30 percent return, but all my friend got out of the deal was wiped out of her savings. Rumors are exactly that: rumors.

Now, if you were standing near a cliff, and all of a sudden a hundred people ran to the edge and jumped, would you do it, too? No. So don't go with (2). You're not a sheep. Don't engage in the herd mentality. Public opinion isn't always right; in fact, it's often wrong. Believe those few people who've earned your trust. Not the hoi polloi (I've always wanted to speak Greek).

Remember: Your money is as personal as your health. Maybe you're investing for the long term, while your 75-year-old cousin is looking for something more short-term. Maybe you need Treasury bills to balance your account, when for someone else investing in

Treasuries would be a mistake. If seven people come down with a cold, *you* don't have to sneeze.

Please, please, please, don't tell me you picked (3). This is called insider trading and you go to jail for it. Yes, other people might get away with cheating and lying and deceiving. That doesn't mean you will. Anyway, could you sleep at night knowing your bed was paid for by dishonesty?

Once again, I wouldn't recommend any of these answers. Be happy your portfolio is doing well, make sure your assets are well allocated, tell you sister's best friend to be careful, and don't take any wooden nickels.

Final Score:

Give yourself a point for the following answers:

1. 3
2. 2
3. (none)
4. 2
5. 2
6. 3
7. (none)

Subtract one point for any other answer.

6–7 points: What are you waiting for? You're psychologically ready to get going. Congratulations!

3–6 points: You have some good instincts, and you have others that still need work. Go back and reread the quiz until you understand where you went wrong; then you'll be ready to invest.

Less than 3: You need to go right to my Web site (http://www.judyresnick.com) and talk to me directly. Now!

3

THREE SAMPLE FINANCIAL PLANS FOR THREE WOMEN

Although investment management now occupies most of my time, in the past my staff and I have worked with hundreds of women on financial planning. The following examples are derived from conversations we had with three of the women who came to see my team. (Of course, we've disguised the women's names and identities, since your financial planner should be just as confidential as your lawyer, psychiatrist, or any other professional adviser.)

What you'll see here are the stories of three different women, one in her thirties, one in her forties, and one in her fifties, and some of the issues we encountered while discussing their financial lives. The form they filled out is the same one I want you to fill out (on page 84), because that's the first step in getting yourself on the right financial track: putting everything you know about your money down on paper, and examining the results.

And believe me, sometimes those results can be a little alarming. But alarm can be a good thing, if it wakes you up to the truth. Know what you have, know what you spend, and then you'll know who you are, financially speaking. So many women don't bother to do that.

For instance, I once spent a day with Lara, a woman worth more than a million dollars. This I had no problem with. My problem was that Lara used to be much richer. Why? Lara shrugged. Bad management, she said. And that can happen, so I gave her my sympathy and told her I was glad she had taken some action to correct her situation.

But when we went over Lara's finances, she told us she scrupulously kept her expenses to a frugal $7,000 a month. Frugal? Maybe when she had two million that was the right amount to spend. But not with the money she had now.

Worse, when we went over all her receipts, we discovered that Lara was actually spending $10,000 a month. Impossible! she said. Ridiculous! She knew how much money was flowing out of her wallet.

Except we had the written proof right in front of us. This woman knew what she was spending on her basic needs, but she seemed to think that those extras, those one-time purchases, didn't matter. You mean, she asked, that first-class airplane ticket to London? That week at the World's Most Expensive Spa?

For some reason, Lara blanked out the big gifts to herself. Perhaps she felt guilt when she spent that kind of money, or perhaps she didn't want to think about it. Nonetheless, she had to face reality: She couldn't splurge and keep her capital intact at the same time.

So now we've got her on a budget, with the promise that next year she'll come in with a more reasonable sense of her cash flow.

I can't tell you how many women will swear that they didn't spend the money, even when they've got the receipts in front of them, complete with their signature. Please: Pay attention to what you spend. The Buddhists say, act mindfully, or in other words, understand the consequences of everything you do. I say, spend mindfully. And save mindfully. Be mindful about your money, and you'll have more money to mind.

Now let me show you the inside story of these three women's finances.

Joanne

Joanne is a close friend of a friend; 50 years old, she's a self-employed attorney with a thriving practice in civil law near Chicago. She has two lovely daughters, Janie and Julie, ages 20 and

17; Janie is a sophomore at Northwestern University, and Julie a high school junior who plans to go to a state college.

Jim, Joanne's husband and the girls' father, died ten years ago of a heart attack. The couple had enjoyed a solid, happy marriage, and Jim's death was a shock to all.

Joanne makes a very comfortable living at $200,000 a year, which is much more than Jim ever made. Although talented, as a sculptor, he had a difficult time in the tough world of art. But Jim loved his work (as did Joanne, who said she married him because of the amazing things he could create with his hands). The issue of who earned more than whom was never a problem for them. I know plenty of other couples for whom the discrepancy might have spelled disaster.

Joanne's investments add another $21,000 to her annual income. So you'd expect Joanne would have few money-related worries.

Unfortunately, that wasn't the case—because, as we soon discovered when Joanne filled out the form on page 31, she spends every penny she makes.

The first question on the agenda was: What did she want to accomplish from this financial consultation and future planning?

Joanne's answer was that she was concerned about her retirement, now that it was only fifteen years away. "Fifteen years!" she said, "Yet I feel as though I were still a young girl. Where does all the time go?"

That question no one could answer for her. But I told her we'd be more helpful with some of her other issues.

She shared them with us. "I have to pay for college for the girls," she said, "although, thank goodness, Julie wants to go to the University of Illinois. And I'm worried about my investments. I know they're not large, but I still feel as if they should be making more money than they do."

We then went over a few more questions: At what age would Joanne like to be financially independent? "Sixty-five," she said. Which is also the age when she'd like to retire.

However, so far she'd only invested $45,000 toward that goal, which means that if she had to retire today, and could somehow pull in 10 percent on that money, after taxes she'd have about $375 a month. That wouldn't even pay her lunch bills.

Joanne currently has another $350,000 that was left to her

when her husband died. She never touched these funds, and certainly never earmarked them for retirement. This investment portfolio includes $50,000 in a bank CD (certificate of deposit), which is earning her 5.5 percent a year. She also has $200,000 in Treasury bills, and another $100,000 in municipal bonds, because she thought these were safe investments, not paying attention to the fact that they don't give her the kind of return she yearns for.

As mentioned, Joanne now has $45,000 in her IRA, since she's been contributing $2,000 a year to it for about fifteen years. This represents her entire savings toward her retirement. In other words, Joanne has now saved less than a quarter of her yearly salary. Even she knows that this isn't an impressive figure for someone of her age and salary level. Joanne will need to include her $350,000 in investments as part of her retirement portfolio and invest for long-term growth.

Joanne owns her home, and there's about $180,000 left on her mortgage.

All this sounds okay, except that as we went over Joanne's monthly budget, we discovered that while Joanne is able to save her investment income, otherwise she spends every penny she makes.

The bottom line: Not only does Joanne indulge herself, but she can't say no to her girls. Between the $80,400 lifestyle expenses we uncovered, the $21,000 annual mortgage payments, and the $30,000 per year education expenses, there was just enough left to pay a rather hefty tax bill.

Now, I have nothing against spending money—when you have it. I love being pampered and having nice things as much as the next woman, but for goodness' sake, be reasonable. Is it really pampering yourself to spend all your disposable income on clothes and have nothing left for your retirement? If someone else played a trick like that on you, you'd consider her irresponsible. And that's really what Joanne was, even as smart as she was, and with such a good career: irresponsible. Remember the fable of the grasshopper and the ant? The grasshopper had fun all summer long, but the industrious ant had stored away enough food that when winter came, he was prepared, while the poor grasshopper had nothing. It's the same with people. If you have fun all through your youth, where do you think your money will come from when you're older? Be an ant.

Joanne, to her credit, understood that things had to change. I admire someone who can see reason where others would dissolve into denial. Joanne was too smart for that. She admitted she'd been too profligate, and wanted to chart a new course.

We then looked over her investments. They weren't a pretty picture, either, yielding just about a 6 percent return before taxes. This came from a conservative mix of bonds and CDs. If Joanne had a much more efficient and broadly diversified portfolio, the total return on the investments could be increased to something closer to 7 or 8 percent before taxes. And if she had a more tax-efficient portfolio, the return could be even higher.

Still, a higher return on her investments wouldn't provide enough to finance Joanne's retirement needs. I told her—as nicely as I could—that she was going to have to make some changes. I pointed out that she was spending about $4,250 a month, or over $50,000 a year, on her mortgage and her education expenses alone. Given that Joanne was going to have to reduce her expenses, one possibility we came up with was to refinance the mortgage on her home. Her interest rate was considerably higher than today's low ones, so we recommended that she go ahead and refinance. And because beginning in about a year both her daughters were going to be in college at the same time, we thought that it would be wise to use the equity on her home to take advantage of the tax deduction on the mortgage interest.

Our ultimate goal would be to have Joanne's mortgage paid off in fifteen years, at retirement. That way, she could then choose to live in her house with a minimum of expenses, or sell it and use the money to rent a home, or buy elsewhere for less, using the difference to add to her retirement account. Let's see how we might accomplish this goal:

By refinancing the first mortgage at competitive rates, and even increasing it to $200,000, Joanne's new monthly payments would be $1,800. (Increasing the current mortgage by $20,000 will help to defray next year's college costs.) To fund the rest of the college costs, we suggested taking out a second mortgage of $100,000 which could be drawn on as needed. Even if this entire amount was borrowed in one year to prepay her daughters' complete college tuition, the monthly payments for a fifteen-year, fully amortized loan on the $100,000 would be only about $925 a month. The total monthly payments on these new mortgages, $2,725, comes to $32,700 per year. Compared to the $51,000 she's spending now ($30,000 per year on tuition and $21,000 on her old mortgage),

Joanne would see an annual cash flow savings of $18,300 during the girls' college years.

Having restructured Joanne's cash flow as outlined above, about $10,000 of her payments represents increased home-mortgage interest. In her tax bracket, this would produce another $3,700 in annual tax savings. Total annual savings implemented by this strategy: $22,000.

(I love my financial planning guy, Joel Framson, a CPA at Glowacki Framson Financial Advisors. He has so much fun adding up these figures, and I have so much fun telling people the results.)

We also suggested that Joanne consider creating a retirement plan for her law practice. Even a simple combination profit sharing and pension plan would permit her to contribute $30,000 per year. While arrangements such as a defined-benefit plan would allow her to put even more away, we began by going over the numbers to convince her that the $30,000 goal could indeed be accomplished.

Here's how: Let's say Joanne reduces her salary to $170,000 in order to make this contribution from her existing business cash flow. The first threshold would be whether she could live on the $170,000, less taxes. Lowering her salary by $30,000 would reduce Joanne's federal taxes by about $11,000. So, without yet reducing her cost of living, but solely with the refinancing and this retirement plan contribution, Joanne would have her annual expenses reduced by slightly more than $33,000. So here we provided a way for Joanne to save more by contributing $30,000 per year to her retirement plan, while still funding her daughters' college costs and continuing her current life-style.

Joanne has to pay attention to a lot of numbers, but it's important that she does.

However, all these savings don't mean she can still afford to buy that extra mink coat and that month's vacation in Paris. Some expense-cutting has to take place. Working with Joanne and her budget, we were able to trim $10,000 of its fat and divert that to savings. On pages 38 and 39 you can see we that we were able to cut $800 from her movie costs (she says she seldom likes those big Hollywood flicks anyway—they're much better on the tube, where you can turn the sound down when the special effects get too overwhelming), $4,000 from her clothing allowance, and so on.

Finally, we reviewed Joanne's business operations and the number of hours she was working. It turned out that Joanne's billable hours were at least 10 percent lower than she thought. With a slight adjustment in her routine, after taxes Joanne should be able to take home another $10,000.

We were then able to do some retirement projections to see how these adjustments would enable Joanne to meet her goals. At the starting point (see page 30, Run 1) we saw a pretty bleak picture. Between the likelihood that inflation would cause the cost of living to soar during Joanne's retirement years, and the fact that her current portfolio choices weren't even keeping up with inflation, it was evident that she'd run out of money only a few years following her retirement.

By increasing the growth of her portfolio to produce a modest 6.5 percent return after taxes, adding the $30,000 retirement plan into the projection, and slightly reducing her lifestyle expenses, we figured that Joanne's retirement funds could be made to last through her eighties.

Due to good genetic factors in Joanne's family, and fact that she's always believed in her heart she'd live a long life, she felt our projections stopped short. By adding $20,000 to her personal savings during her working years, we're now able to project that there will be a healthy retirement fund available even at age 90. As mentioned, considering that the house mortgage will be paid off by the time she's 65, Joanne should look forward to owning an expensive home that she could either leave as an inheritance to her kids, or sell to obtain that much more money to last her well into her second century!

All in all, now that Joanne has decided to get her financial act together, she's in good shape. I love it when people leave my office happy.

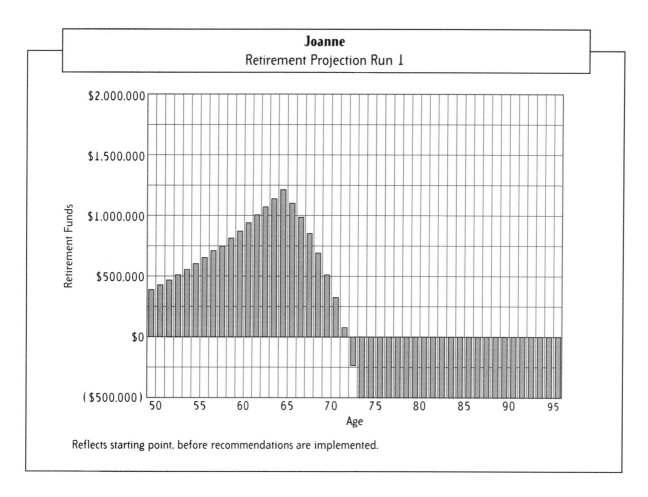

Joanne
Retirement Projection Run 1

Reflects starting point, before recommendations are implemented.

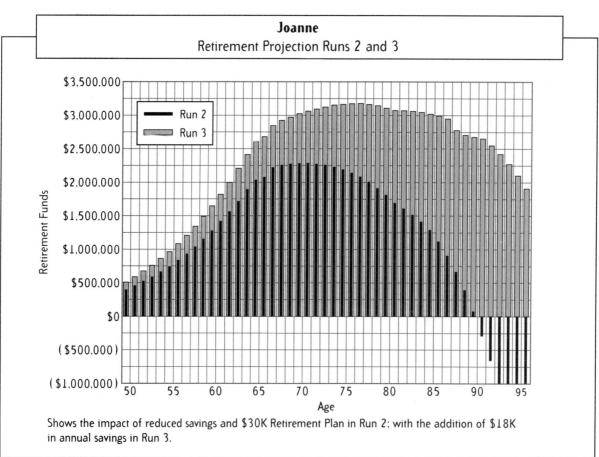

Joanne
Retirement Projection Runs 2 and 3

Shows the impact of reduced savings and $30K Retirement Plan in Run 2; with the addition of $18K in annual savings in Run 3.

Confidential Information Worksheet

Personal Information

Date ___5/1___

Client name(s) and age(s) _Joanne — 50_

Address _____

Phone numbers:

    Business _____ Home _____

Occupation:

    Self _Attorney_____ Spouse _____

Family Information

Enter your dependents' names and dates of birth:

Name	Birth date (or age)
Janie (college sophomore)	20
Julie (high school junior)	17

What do you want to accomplish from this financial consultation and future planning?

_Retirement_____

_College for Julie_____

_____

Do you have any short-term goals, e.g., buying a new home or boat, that would be relevant to your financial planning?

_College_____

_____

_____

Financial Independence

At what age do you plan to be financially independent?   _65_

At what age would you ideally like to retire?   _65_

How much monthly income is needed to retire comfortably?   _$5625_
(in today's economy?)

How much have you invested to date for retirement?   _$45,000_

How much will your company retirement plan pay?   _n/a_

What plans have you made to date about retirement?

few

Estate Planning Information

In the event of your death, how much annual income is needed for your family:

Until your youngest child is out of high school?   _n/a_

For your spouse after the children are grown?   _n/a_

Amount saved for your children's education?   _0_

Cost annually for each child's undergraduate study?   _$20,000_

Cost annually for graduate studies?   _n/a_

I have (a) plan (s) for my practice/business at death   Y _____ N _✓_ N/A _____

Do both spouses have a will/trust?   Y _____   N _✓_

Life and Disability Insurance Benefits

What is the face amount of your life insurance?   _1.5 M_

What is the amount of insurance on your spouse?   _n/a_

Amount of insurance provided by your company?   _n/a_

Disability benefits at work or from a personal policy?   _personal_

How much? $6000/mo.

How much in liquid emergency funds are needed? $32-40,000

Financial Assets and Debts

(Attach copy of recent statement showing details where applicable)

	Value	Market Annual Rate of Return/ Growth Rate
Personal Liquid Assets		
Checking accounts	$ _____	_____ %
Certificates of deposit	$ 50,000	5.5 %
Stocks	$ _____	_____ %
Bonds—taxable	$ 200,000	7 %
Bonds—tax-free	$ 100,000	4 %
Mutual funds	$ _____	_____ %
Other	$ _____	_____ %
Other	$ _____	_____ %
Other	$ _____	_____ %
Retirement Plan Assets		
IRA accounts	$ 45,000	5.5 %
Self-employed plan	$ _____	_____ %
Company retirement plans	$ _____	_____ %
Other	$ _____	_____ %

Real Estate	Value	Mortgage Balance
Residence	$ 500,000	180,000
Vacation/second residence	$ _____	_____
Rental	$ _____	_____

Business or Practice Value

_____ $ _n/a_____

_____ $ _____

Debts

	Unpaid Balance
Investment loans (other than real estate)	$ _O_____
Consumer debts (autos, charge accts., etc.)	$ _O_____

Personal Treadmill
Statement of Cash Flow

For the year ended December 31, _____

Personal Income	Monthly Estimate	Annual Estimate
Salary, wages, tips		_200,000_
Pension retirement/income		
Social security		
Other personal income		
Total personal income (A)		_200,000_

Business/Investment Income		
Business income		
Rent/royalty income		
Interest/dividend income		_21,000_
Other investment income		
Total bus./inv. income (B)		_21,000_
Total Income (A + B = C)		_221,000_

Personal Expenses

	Monthly Estimate	Annual Estimate
Living expenses (*from page 38*)		80,400
Personal income taxes		70,000
Social security taxes		(included)
Education expenses		30,000
Personal-debt service:		
Mortgage principal and interest	1750	21,000
Other interest		
Other expenses		
Total personal expenses (D)		201,400

Business/Investment Expenses

	Monthly Estimate	Annual Estimate
Business/investment income taxes		
Investment-debt service:		
Principal		
Interest		
Other bus./inv. expenses		
Total bus./inv. expenses (E)		n/a
Total Expenses (D + E = F)		201,400
Cash available for long-term uses (C-F)		19,600

Treadmill Living Expenses

Recreation

	Monthly Estimate	Annual Estimate
Dining out		4000
Movies		2000
Recreation		
Vacations		2000
Hobbies		2000
Country club		
Summer camp		
Sporting events		
Entertaining		2000

Transportation

	Monthly Estimate	Annual Estimate
Auto lease		7200
Gasoline		1000
Public transportation		1200
Parking & tolls		
Maintenance/repairs		1000
License plates & fees		400

Household

	Monthly Estimate	Annual Estimate
Rent		
Condo/assoc. fees		
Gas & electricity		1200
Telephone		2000
Household maintenance		2000
Water & sewage		
Groceries		5000

	Monthly Estimate	Annual Estimate
Child care		
Clothing		10,000
Lawn care		1500

Gifts

	Monthly Estimate	Annual Estimate
Birthdays		1000
Holidays		1500
Anniversaries		
Special occasions		

Miscellaneous

	Monthly Estimate	Annual Estimate
Barber/beauty parlor		3000
Dry cleaning		3000
Newspapers/subscriptions		
Pet care		
Domestic help		4000
Allowances		1000
Adult care		
Lessons		
Cosmetics & personal care		1000
Other		

Itemized Deductions

	Monthly Estimate	Annual Estimate
Medicine & medical bills		1000
Property taxes		8000
Cash charitable contributions		3000
Other itemized deductions		

	Monthly Estimate	Annual Estimate

Insurance Premiums

	Monthly Estimate	Annual Estimate
Auto		1500
Homeowners		1500
Disability		4000
Health		
Life		2000
Personal liability		400
Other insurance		
Total Living Expenses		80,400

Adjusted Treadmill Living Expenses

For those looking to hold down expenses, we use this list to help you figure out where you can cut back. First put down under column A what you spend on each item (from the Annual Estimate column above). Then, in column B, write down what you think you could spend if you were willing to save a little. If this gets you to where you'd like to be in terms of budget, then you can stop. Otherwise, try again with column C, saving still a little more. Then write down your adjusted total on the final line.

Recreation

	A List	B List	C List	Adj. Total
Dining out	4000	3000	2000	2000
Movies	2000	1200	800	1200
Recreation				
Vacations	2000	1000		1000
Hobbies	2000	1000		1000
Country club				
Summer camp				

	A List	B List	C List	Adj. Total
Sporting events				
Entertaining	2000		1000	1000

Transportation

	A List	B List	C List	Adj. Total
Auto lease	7200			7200
Gasoline	1000			1000
Public transportation	1200	1200		1200
Parking & tolls				
Maintenance/repairs	1000			1000
License plates & fees	400			400

Household

	A List	B List	C List	Adj. Total
Rent				
Condo/assoc. fees				
Gas & electricity	1200			1200
Telephone	2000	2000		2000
Household maintenance	2000	2000		2000
Water & sewage				
Groceries	5000	5000		5000
Child care				
Clothing	10,000	6000	5000	6000
Lawn care	1500	1500		1500

Gifts

	A List	B List	C List	Adj. Total
Birthdays	1000	600		600
Holidays	1500	1000	500	1500
Anniversaries				
Special occasions				

Miscellaneous

	A List	B List	C List	Adj. Total
Barber/beauty parlor	3000	2000		2800
Dry cleaning	3000	2000	1000	3000
Newspapers/subscriptions				
Pet care				
Domestic help	4000	2000	2000	3000
Allowances	1000		1000	1000
Adult care				
Lessons				
Cosmetics & personal care	1000			500
Other				

Itemized Deductions

	A List	B List	C List	Adj. Total
Medicine & medical bills	1000			1000
Property taxes	8000			8000
Cash charitable contrib.	3000	2000	1000	2000
Other itemized deductions				

Insurance Premiums

	A List	B List	C List	Adj. Total
Auto	1500			1500
Homeowners	1500			1500
Disability	4000			4000
Health				
Life	2000			2000
Person Liability	400			400
Other Insurance				

	A List	B List	C List	Adj. Total
Total Adjusted Treadmill Living Expenses	80,400			67,500

Marcy

Thirty-three-year-old Marcy, whom I discussed in my first book, was recently divorced from her husband, Ted. They'd been married for about ten years; Marcy was a high school teacher when she first met Ted, and she left her job to raise their two kids, who are now eight and ten years old. The couple has joint custody.

In the divorce settlement Marcy was awarded a lump sum of $250,000, along with the house and child support payments of $900 per month. The divorce was pretty unpleasant, because Ted was running off with his secretary, Mollie. Mollie's and Marcy's mothers were friends, and Marcy had helped place Mollie in her job. Marcy and Mollie no longer speak (neither do their mothers).

Marcy decided to go back to teaching school, which she really loves. Her salary is up to $36,000 a year now.

Unlike most of the women I meet, Marcy is very comfortable with numbers—she teaches mathematics and is the chaperon of the school's math club. But she was never involved in any of the family's financial or investment decisions. Ted always told her that it was his duty to take care of these things. Marcy now wonders whether he meant that it was a chore from which he was saving her, or that he was casting aspersions on her ability to understand money.

Regardless, now that Marcy's on her own, she's hesitant to pick up a responsibility that Ted never let her have.

"But you're probably more relaxed about numbers than almost anyone I've worked with," I said.

Marcy shook her head. "It's not about the math," she said. "It's the idea that I have to do any of this in the first place. I guess I always believed that was one reason why you got married—so that someone else would do this."

Naturally this lead to a long detour about men and women, love and marriage, and relationships and divorce.

Once we were back looking at Marcy's file, we continued. As you can see from the figures on page 44, Run 1, if Marcy were simply to invest her settlement using a conservative strategy, she'd run into problems with taxes and inflation, and would eventually have nothing left.

So we all sat down and talked about how Marcy could best take care of her money and her family.

First, Marcy needs to have an idea of what she's spending, so we can all get a sense of her current life-style.

After she'd completed her worksheet (page 45), it became evident that she was going to have to supplement her salary with some investment income. On the whole, however, her income and expenses seem to balance.

Still, she'll need to keep track of her budgeting for some time, until it becomes natural for her to do this sort of thing.

To give Marcy some additional financial comfort, we thought she should take part of her settlement and set it aside in a savings account as an emergency fund. I didn't see any reason why she should need more than about $20,000 in this fund, since she's got quite a bit of equity in her home which could be tapped in an emergency—almost $200,000 in fact. And if she uses a good savings vehicle, she could be able to generate a return of about 5 percent on this $20,000 fund—$1000 of income she can use to supplement the rest of her money.

Marcy's school offers a deferred-salary savings plan; they'll match 50 percent of up to the first $3,000 Marcy elects to save. But at her current salary of $36,000, Marcy can really only afford to defer about $1,600, based on her monthly living expenses.

Again, here are some numbers to think about: Marcy's salary is in the 15 percent tax bracket; if she reduces it by an even $2,000, she'll save $400 on her income taxes. Since this $400 savings, added to the available $1,600, will keep her expenses covered and will take advantage of $1,000 that her employer will contribute to the plan as a match, it makes sense for Marcy to put the money away.

Now, in order for Joel Framson, our numbers guy, to project Marcy's current spending level throughout her retirement years, Marcy needs to increase her portfolio growth rate. If she's comfortable with an asset allocation that will provide her a minimum return of 6.5 percent after taxes, she should be able to retire at a normal retirement age with adequate security (see page 44, Runs 2 and 3). This would mean, however, that $7500 of Marcy's total investment income of $8500 would have to be reinvested, and would not be available for spending.

Since ex-husband Ted is obliged to pay for half of the state college tuition cost for their kids, Marcy, too, only pays half. We projected these education costs and determined when they're due, which enabled Marcy to see that she'd be able to meet this obligation easily. This relieved her no end. Sometimes people don't volunteer their worst fear, so it's only when you tell them they don't have to worry and they breathe a huge sigh of relief that you know you've hit their hot spot. In Marcy's case, her biggest fear was that when it came time for the kids to go to school, she'd have to plead with Ted to pay more than his share. There's no question: Money and emotions are inextricably linked.

In doing these calculations, we didn't consider Marcy's home equity—the money she would make if she sold her house—as a current asset, because the reality is that she doesn't want to sell it. But that equity is substantial, and could provide some additional income if Marcy really needed it. In 1997 the government changed the rules governing taxation of primary residences, so Marcy should be able to sell the house when she's ready, and pay no taxes on the gain. At that time, she might be able to reduce her mortgage payment, if not eliminate it altogether, by moving into a rental, and thus have additional funds to invest. That's all part of why I feel that for many people, owning a home is a wonderful thing: Not only do you get a place to live, but you get an emergency fund if you need it some day.

Next we drifted on to some other issues. One thing that I reminded Marcy: Now that she's divorced, she needs to draft a new will. Even if her children are the beneficiaries of her estate, she'll have to name a guardian for them while they're minors—and that's something that Marcy needs to address as soon as possible.

Finally, Marcy has a $100,000 term life insurance policy. We had a long talk about whether or not this was sufficient. Between the equity in her house and the lump-sum settlement, she may determine that no additional insurance is required. Still, we told her that she should discuss this matter with a qualified insurance specialist.

Then we had a long talk about her future. I was impressed that Marcy was willing to admit that while she wanted to be in a relationship again, she might never find Mr. Right, and she's ready to lead a full, rewarding life no matter what happens. Her most important goal is to take good care of herself and her kids. Meeting people like Marcy always makes me feel better.

Marcy
Retirement Projection Run 1

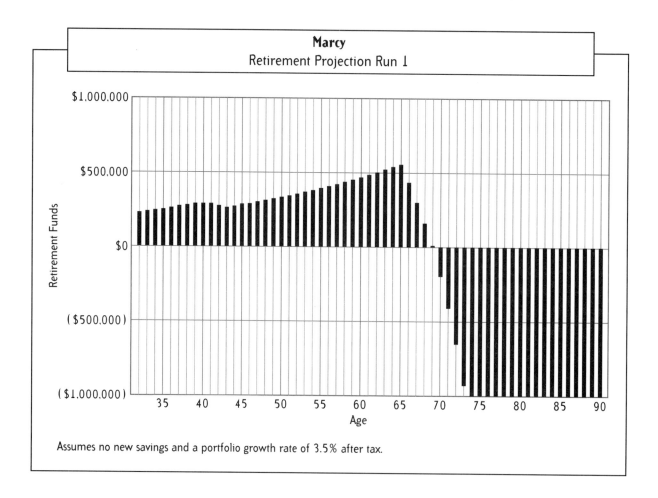

Assumes no new savings and a portfolio growth rate of 3.5% after tax.

Marcy
Retirement Projection Runs 2 and 3

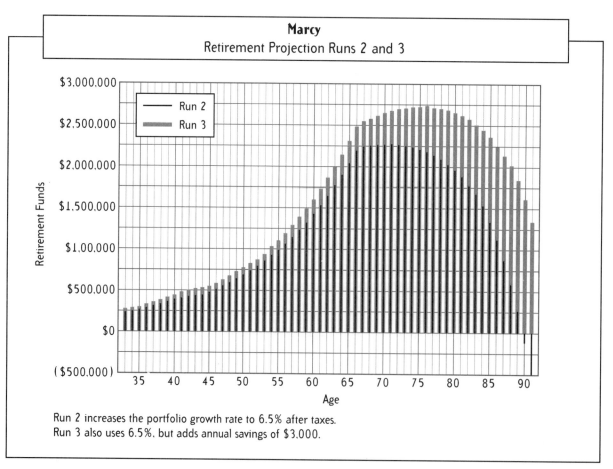

Run 2 increases the portfolio growth rate to 6.5% after taxes.
Run 3 also uses 6.5%, but adds annual savings of $3,000.

Confidential Information Worksheet

Personal Information

Date ___11/12___

Client name(s) and age(s) _Marcy Age 33_

Address _Los Angeles_

Phone numbers:

    Business _____ Home _____

Occupation:

    Self _H.S. Teacher_____ Spouse _____

Family Information

Enter your dependents' names and dates of birth:

Name	Birth date (or age)
Ted, Jr.	10
Jessica	8

What do you want to accomplish from this financial consultation and future planning?

    Just divorced, looking for financial security

    Want to plan for retirement, children's education

Do you have any short-term goals, e.g., buying a new home or boat, that would be relevant to your financial planning?

    Need to feel comfortable being on my own

    Need to know how to plan and handle my finances

Financial Independence

At what age do you plan to be financially independent?   Never

At what age would you ideally like to retire?   65

How much monthly income is needed to retire comfortably? $2250

(in today's economy?)

How much have you invested to date for retirement?   0

How much will your company retirement plan pay?   Annual match of 50% up to $3000

What plans have you made to date about retirement?

Estate Planning Information

In the event of your death, how much annual income is needed for your family:

Until your youngest child is out of high school?   their father would take custody

For your spouse after the children are grown?   n/a

Amount saved for your children's education?   0

Cost annually for each child's undergraduate study?   12,000

Cost annually for graduate studies?   n/a

I have (a) plan(s) for my practice/business at death   Y _____ N _____ N/A ✔

Do both spouses have a will/trust?   Y _____ N ✔

Life and Disability Insurance Benefits

What is the face amount of your life insurance?   100,000

What is the amount of insurance on your spouse?   n/a

Amount of insurance provided by your company?   10,000

Disability benefits at work or from a personal policy?   _n/a_____

How much?   _____

How much in liquid emergency funds are needed?   ___20,000_____

Financial Assets and Debts

(Attach copy of recent statement showing details where applicable)

Personal Liquid Assets

	Value	Market Annual Rate of Return/ Growth Rate
Checking accounts	$ _____	_____ %
Certificates of deposit	$ _250,000____	__3.4____ %
Stocks	$ _____	_____ %
Bonds—taxable	$ _____	_____ %
Bonds—tax-free	$ _____	_____ %
Mutual funds	$ _____	_____ %
Other	$ _____	_____ %
Other	$ _____	_____ %
Other	$ _____	_____ %

Retirement Plan Assets

	Value	Market Annual Rate of Return/ Growth Rate
IRA accounts	$ _____	_____ %
Self-employed plan	$ _____	_____ %
Company retirement plans	$ _____	_____ %
Other	$ _____	_____ %

Real Estate

	Value	Mortgage Balance
Residence	$ 400,000	200,000
Vacation/second residence	$ _____	_____
Rental	$ _____	

Business or Practice Value

	$ __n/a__
	$ ____

Debts

	Unpaid Balance
Investment loans (other than real estate)	$ __0__
Consumer debts (autos, charge accts., etc.)	$ __0__

Personal Treadmill
Statement of Cash Flow

For the year ended December 31, _____

Personal Income	Monthly Estimate	Annual Estimate
Salary, wages, tips		36,000
Pension retirement/income		
Social security		
Other personal income	900	10,800
Total personal income (A)		46,800

Business/Investment Income		
Business income		
Rent/royalty income		
Interest/dividend income		8,500
Other investment income		
Total bus./inv. income (B)		
Total Income (A + B = C)		55,300

(less investment income not available for spending) -7,500

47,800

Personal Expenses

	Monthly Estimate	Annual Estimate
Living expenses (*from page 52*)		25,600
Personal income taxes		1850
Social security taxes		3150
Education expenses		
Personal-debt service:		
Mortgage principal and interest	1300	15,600
Other interest		
Other expenses		
Total personal expenses (D)		

Business/Investment Expenses

	Monthly Estimate	Annual Estimate
Business/investment income taxes		
Investment-debt service:		
Principal		
Interest		
Other bus./inv. expenses		
Total bus./inv. expenses (E)		n/a
Total Expenses (D + E = F)		46,200
Cash available for long-term uses (C-F)		1600

Treadmill Living Expenses

Recreation	Monthly Estimate	Annual Estimate
Dining out		400
Movies		400
Recreation		400
Vacations		
Hobbies		
Country club		
Summer camp		
Sporting events		
Entertaining		

Transportation		
Auto lease		
Gasoline		500
Public transportation		
Parking & tolls		
Maintenance/repairs		400
License plates & fees		200

Household		
Rent		
Condo/assoc. fees		
Gas & electricity		1800
Telephone		1200
Household maintenance		1200
Water & sewage		
Groceries		6000

	Monthly Estimate	Annual Estimate
Child care		
Clothing		2000
Lawn care		

Gifts

	Monthly Estimate	Annual Estimate
Birthdays		300
Holidays		1000
Anniversaries		
Special occasions		200

Miscellaneous

	Monthly Estimate	Annual Estimate
Barber/beauty parlor		300
Dry cleaning		200
Newspapers/subscriptions		100
Pet care		
Domestic help		
Allowances		200
Adult care		
Lessons		
Cosmetics & personal care		200
Other		

Itemized Deductions

	Monthly Estimate	Annual Estimate
Medicine & medical bills		2000
Property taxes		4000
Cash charitable contributions		
Other itemized deductions		

	Monthly Estimate	Annual Estimate

Insurance Premiums

	Monthly Estimate	Annual Estimate
Auto		1400
Homeowners		1200
Disability		
Health		
Life		
Personal liability		
Other insurance		
Total Living Expenses		25,600

Adjusted Treadmill Living Expenses

Since we didn't need to do any serious work on Marcy's living expenses, we didn't feel the need to fill out her Adjusted Treadmill Living Expenses form.

Susan and Bill

Susan, who arrived in my office along with her husband, Bill, is another friend of a friend. She and Bill, both forty, have been married for fifteen years, and theirs is the kind of marriage that gives the word its good name. It's not that they don't have issues, but what makes their marriage enviable is the way they handle them. The couple sit down and try to make things better, rather than blame each other, heave around insults, or generally act in ways that lead to divorce rather than to love. Frankly, I admire them both.

Bill is a software designer, and Susan, who was once an advertising executive, is now at home, raising their two kids, aged 12 and 10. Susan and Bill are doing well financially: Bill has his own business, and after expenses he nets about $150,000 a year—and that figure has been rising steadily.

Their agenda was clear: They both wanted Susan to become more familiar with the family finances, and they wanted to gain some confidence about their retirement and their financial future in general. Bill's business is growing, but he's been working hard for many years, and he'd love to stop at age 62, if possible. Bill's father recently died of a heart attack, and Bill has visions of mortality floating before him.

Another goal, admittedly based on their friends' achievements and on the successes of Bill's older brothers, is to achieve financial independence by the time Bill reaches the age of 55. Bill looked almost sheepish when he admitted this, but I applauded him; if you've made enough money so that you don't have to work, and you don't want to, why continue?

Bill and Susan keep good records, so we went over all the that we could (see 58). Immediately we noticed that, like nearly everyone else in America, Susan and Bill are spending more than they should: Their expenses are about $5,600 a year more than they make.

Consequently, instead of adding to their retirement savings, they're adding to their credit-card debt.

Bill is certain that his business will soon become more profitable. He dreams of the day his employees will do most of his work, freeing him to make long-range strategic planning decisions, and then, beyond that, the day when he can semi-retire and let the business run itself.

Well, I said, we all dream. Dreams are great. I love to dream, awake or asleep. Just don't operate as though dreams represent reality. Yes, some day Bill may make a great deal more money. But there's no victory in spending the money just yet. Bill can't afford to wait before making some solid lifestyle changes that will permit him to increase his savings—whether or not his business takes off.

For instance, one immediate solution we came up with to defray the high interest on their credit-card debt was to take out a $20,000 home equity line of credit. By paying off their entire credit-card debt, they would save approximately $250 a month. Also, since the home equity line of credit payment on the house would be tax deductible, it creates an annual tax savings of more than $500. With these adjustments, Susan and Bill would save about $3,500 each year.

Next we talked about their budget, something they had seldom discussed with each other. Using their Personal Treadmill Statement of Cash Flow, they had to decide which of their expenses were essential, which were next most important and necessary, and which were basically discretionary and therefore could be eliminated—or at least, cut back considerably.

After kicking these numbers around, we came up with several areas where the couple could cut back enough to lower their annual expenses. They chose to reduce their spending on these items: gifts to each other, which were running over $6,000 a year; entertaining, since Susan admitted she really didn't like having large parties anyway; and vacations—the family had been spending $10,000 a year on two fourteen-day trips, and they decided that from now on they'd take just one vacation a year. They even toyed with the idea of going camping, although the kids didn't seem thrilled about that one. I said, tell the kids it's either a pup tent or college. (Well, not exactly—but they knew what I meant.)

These savings reduced the family's spending by $16,000 a year.

And when we looked harder, we found ways to leverage this amount even more. Since Bill is self-employed, we decided he should investigate whether a different type of company retirement plan would permit him to contribute more than the current $10,000 limit on 401K deductions. Consider this tax-saving scenario, Joel Framson said: Bill's company starts a new defined-contribution plan that permits him to contribute up to 25 percent of his salary. At the same time, he reduces his paid salary by the $14,300 that is no longer needed for expenses, and contributes this to the new plan, along with the $9,500 that he'd been contributing in prior years.

Two things now occur. The new contribution to Bill's retirement plan becomes $23,800. However, since he reduced his salary by $14,300 and he's in the 31 percent federal income-tax bracket, his income (and social security) taxes are reduced by about $4,600. At this point, Bill could either further reduce his salary and add more to the company retirement plan, or he could personally save this amount.

Bill and Susan's decision was to use $2,000 of this amount as a Roth IRA contribution, and to invest another $2,000 in an after-tax portfolio (see Run 2). Still, even with all these changes, Susan and Bill aren't able to obtain financial independence at age 55. For that, they'd need an additional $40,000 per year.

Bill looked unhappy. "Is there any way at all I could get there?" he asked.

There were only two scenarios we could come up with: One was for Susan to go back to work. With the kids reaching an age where Susan didn't have to stay at home all the time, she could go back into advertising. She may not earn $40,000 a year right off the bat, but any amount she makes and saves would help the couple reach their goal of freedom by 55.

The other option: Should Bill's business takes off as he expects, it's possible that he could increase his salary and company-retirement plan contribution by an average of $40,000 a year during this period, and thereby reach that magical goal.

We did another run on the computer (What did people use before computers? Abacuses?) and found that if Bill is indeed right about his business, he might be able to sell it at age 55.

If he doesn't want to continue working after that time, for how much must he sell the business (after taxes) to enable the couple to live comfortably? It turns out the sale price would need to be at least $1.5 million, assuming a capital-gains tax rate of 18 percent still applies.

How likely is this to happen? Although Bill is optimistic, Susan doesn't want her financial security to depend on whether or not Bill's business can be sold in a decade and a half.

So look at page 57. Here's something that made Susan feel more comfortable. This projection shows what would happen if Bill works for an additional seven years, using all the same assumptions, in Run 62-1. Specifically, he continues to earn the same amount, contribute the same amount to his company retirement plan, and keep the family's living expenses down to $72,000 annually, instead of $88,400. While technically this choice doesn't meet the goal of financial independence by age 55, it does meet the couple's goal of being able to retire by age 62.

After talking about it, both Susan and Bill realized that this wasn't such a big trade-off, as they could conceivably live another 30 or 40 years after that, in which case the seven years of extra work didn't seem so bad.

And, of course, if Bill were to sell the business, or if Susan were to go back to work, then they could reach financial independence that much sooner.

The couple's other concern was their kids' college education. To fund that properly would require saving another $15,000 per year, starting immediately. "But we just figured out how to make everything work out," Bill moaned. I reminded him that no one can figure out the future perfectly, because the future keeps changing. If it didn't, it wouldn't be the future.

Susan and Bill felt that $15,000 a year was too much for them right now, because they were struggling to meet their own retirement goals. So they've decided to put faith in Bill's company succeeding, and putting whatever extra money it makes into a college fund. They're also considering having the kids eventually work part time in the business in order to earn part of these funds at a very low income-tax rate.

One other issue that arose: an emergency fund. Susan felt strongly that the couple should have enough money on hand should some incidental but necessary expense arise. Looking into it, we saw that they currently have sufficient savings from which they can carve out a $24,000 emergency fund, which they'd then keep in a liquid account.

During the planning we also discovered that Bill had neither adequate life insurance nor adequate disability insurance, so we discussed his increasing both.

Perhaps most important, when the session ended, the couple had accomplished their other major goal: getting Susan involved in

Susan and Bill
Age 55 Financial Independence Options

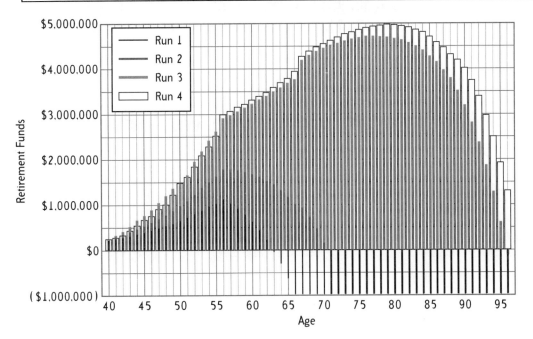

Run 1 is without any new planning ideas. Run 2 reflects cutting expenses and increasing savings, but is not nearly enough. To meet their goals, Run 3 shows annual after-tax savings increasing by $40,000. Another option, shown in Run 4, projects the sale of Bill's business at age 55.

Susan and Bill
Retirement Projection Runs 55-1 and 62-1

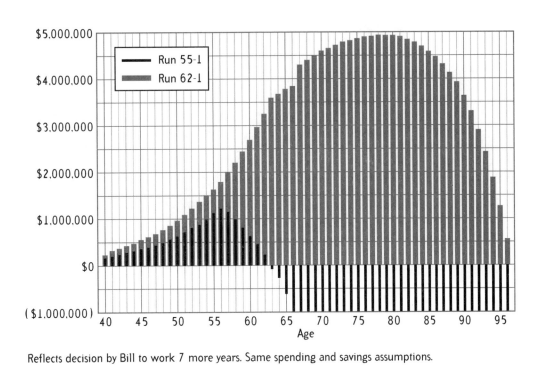

Reflects decision by Bill to work 7 more years. Same spending and savings assumptions.

the family's finances. Susan decided to take over as principal record keeper, meaning that not only did she maintain the receipts and bills, but she became responsible for making sure their wills were up-to-date and in a secure place, and that all their records were conveniently and safely stored.

Confidential Information Worksheet

Personal Information

Date _____5/2_____

Client name(s) and age(s) __Bill and Susan   Age 40_____

Address _____

Phone numbers:

   Business _____ Home _____

Occupation:

   Self _Software Developer_____ Spouse _____Homemaker_____

Family Information

Enter your dependents' names and dates of birth:

Name	Birth date (or age)
Bill, Jr.	12
Heather	10

What do you want to accomplish from this financial consultation and future planning?

   Understand our finances for Susan's comfort and confidence

   about retirement & the future.

   Can Bill retire at 55?

Do you have any short-term goals, e.g., buying a new home or boat, that would be relevant to your financial planning?

College funding

Financial Independence

At what age do you plan to be financially independent?   55

At what age would you ideally like to retire?   62

How much monthly income is needed to retire comfortably? $6000

(in today's economy?)

How much have you invested to date for retirement? $150,000

How much will your company retirement plan pay?   n/a

What plans have you made to date about retirement?

Company retirement plan

Estate Planning Information

In the event of your death, how much annual income is needed for your family:

Until your youngest child is out of high school? $5000

For your spouse after the children are grown? $4000

Amount saved for your children's education?   0

Cost annually for each child's undergraduate study? $15,000

Cost annually for graduate studies?   n/a

I have (a) plan(s) for my practice/business at death   Y _____ N ✔ N/A _____

Do both spouses have a will/trust?   Y ✔ _____ N _____

Life and Disability Insurance Benefits

What is the face amount of your life insurance? _____ 0 _____

What is the amount of insurance on your spouse? _____ 0 _____

Amount of insurance provided by your company? _____ 0 _____

Disability benefits at work or from a personal policy? _____ 0 _____

How much? _____

How much in liquid emergency funds are needed? _____ $24,000 _____

Financial Assets and Debts

(Attach copy of recent statement showing details where applicable)

Personal Liquid Assets

	Value	Market Annual Rate of Return/ Growth Rate
Checking accounts	$ _____	_____ %
Certificates of deposit	$ 10,000	5 %
Stocks	$ 20,000	10 %
Bonds—taxable	$ _____	_____ %
Bonds—tax-free	$ _____	_____ %
Mutual funds (balanced)	$ 15,000	8 %
Other	$ _____	_____ %
Other	$ _____	_____ %
Other	$ _____	_____ %

Retirement Plan Assets

	Value	
IRA accounts	$ _____	_____ %
Self-employed plan	$ _____	_____ %
Company retirement plans	$ 150,000	8 %
Other	$ _____	_____ %

Real Estate

	Value	Mortgage Balance
Residence	$ _200,000_	_140,000_
Vacation/second residence	$ _____	_____
Rental	$ _____	_____

Business or Practice Value

_____	$ _____0_____
_____	$ _____

Debts

	Unpaid Balance
Investment loans (other than real estate)	$ _____0_____
Consumer debts (autos, charge accts., etc.)	$ _40,000 auto (8%)_
	20,000 Visa (17%)

Personal Treadmill
Statement of Cash Flow

For the year ended December 31, _____

Personal Income

	Monthly Estimate	Annual Estimate
Salary, wages, tips	_____	_150,000_
Pension retirement income	_____	_____
Social security	_____	_____
Other personal/income	_____	_____
Total personal income (A)	_____	_150,000_

Business/Investment Income

Business income	_____	_____
Rent/royalty income	_____	_____

	Monthly Estimate	Annual Estimate
Interest/dividend income		1500
Other investment income		
Total bus./inv. income (B)		1500
Total Income (A + B = C)		151,500

Personal Expenses

	Monthly Estimate	Annual Estimate
Living expenses (*from page 65*)		88,400
Personal income taxes		35,000
Social security taxes		6200
Education expenses		
Personal-debt service:		
Mortgage principal and interest		13,200
Other interest		
Other expenses		4800
Total personal expenses (D)		147,600

Business/Investment Expenses

	Monthly Estimate	Annual Estimate
Business/investment income taxes		n/a
Investment-debt service:		
Principal		
Interest		
Other bus./inv. expenses		9500 401K
Total bus./inv. expenses (E)		9500
Total Expenses (D + E = F)		157,100
Cash available for long-term uses (C–F)		-5600

Treadmill Living Expenses

Recreation	Monthly Estimate	Annual Estimate
Dining out		2000
Movies		1000
Recreation		4000
Vacations		10,000
Hobbies		1000
Country club		6000
Summer camp		4000
Sporting events		1000
Entertaining		1000

Transportation		
Auto lease		7800
Gasoline		800
Public transportation		
Parking & tolls		200
Maintenance/repairs		2000
License plates & fees		200

Household		
Rent		
Condo/assoc. fees		
Gas & electricity		2500
Telephone		1200
Household maintenance		2000
Water & sewage		
Groceries		12,000

	Monthly Estimate	Annual Estimate
Child care		1000
Clothing		8000
Lawn care		1200

Gifts

	Monthly Estimate	Annual Estimate
Birthdays		2000
Holidays		2000
Anniversaries		1000
Special occasions		1000

Miscellaneous

	Monthly Estimate	Annual Estimate
Barber/beauty parlor		1000
Dry cleaning		1500
Newspapers/subscriptions		250
Pet care		750
Domestic help		1500
Allowances		1000
Adult care		
Lessons		1000
Cosmetics & personal care		500
Other		

Itemized Deductions

	Monthly Estimate	Annual Estimate
Medicine & medical bills		500
Property taxes		2000
Cash charitable contributions		1000
Other itemized deductions		

Insurance Premiums

	Monthly Estimate	Annual Estimate
Auto		1500
Homeowners		1000
Disability		
Health		
Life		
Personal liability		
Other insurance		
Total Living Expenses		88,400

Adjusted Treadmill Living Expenses

For those looking to hold down expenses, we use this list to help you figure out where you can cut back. First put down under column A what you spend on each item (from the Annual Estimate column above). Then, in column B, write down what you think you could spend if you were willing to save a little. If this gets you to where you'd like to be in terms of budget, then you can stop. Otherwise, try again with column C, saving still a little more. Then write down your adjusted total on the final line.

Recreation

	A List	B List	C List	Adj. Total
Dining out	2000	1500		1500
Movies	1000	500		500
Recreation	4000	3000		3000
Vacations	10,000	5000		5000
Hobbies	1000			1000
Country club	6000	5000		5000
Summer camp	4000			4000

	A List	B List	C List	Adj. Total
Sporting events	1000	500		500
Entertaining	1000	500		500

Transportation

	A List	B List	C List	Adj. Total
Auto lease	7800			7800
Gasoline	800			800
Public transportation				
Parking & tolls	200			200
Maintenance/repairs	2000			2000
License plates & fees	200			200

Household

	A List	B List	C List	Adj. Total
Rent				
Condo/assoc. fees				
Gas & electricity	2500			2500
Telephone	1200			1200
Household maintenance	2000			2000
Water & sewage				
Groceries	12,000	10,000		10,000
Child care	1000			1000
Clothing	8000	6000		6000
Lawn care	1200	800		800

Gifts

	A List	B List	C List	Adj. Total
Birthdays	2000	1500	1000	1000
Holidays	2000	1000		1000
Anniversaries	1000	500		500
Special occasions	1000	500		500

Miscellaneous

	A List	B List	C List	Adj. Total
Barber/beauty parlor	1000			1000
Dry cleaning	1500			1500
Newspapers/subscriptions	250			250
Pet care	750			750
Domestic help	1500			1500
Allowances	1000			1000
Adult care				
Lessons	1000			1000
Cosmetics & personal care	500			500
Other				

Itemized Deductions

	A List	B List	C List	Adj. Total
Medicine & medical bills	500			500
Property taxes	2000			2000
Cash charitable contrib.	1000			1000
Other itemized deductions				

Insurance Premiums

	A List	B List	C List	Adj. Total
Auto	1500			1500
Homeowners	1000			1000
Disability				
Health				
Life				
Person Liability				
Other Insurance				

	A List	B List	C List	Adj. Total
Total Adjusted Treadmill Living Expenses	88,400			72,000

THE BASICS:
GET OUT A PENCIL
AND GET TO WORK

Okay, you've seen what other women have gone through to understand their financial reality. Now it's time to work on your own.

Remember, there is one economic fact of life with which you must come to terms: Only you are responsible for your own economic survival. That's right. You, and you alone. So if you haven't already done so, get your economic act together and take charge.

How do you know whether or not you're not in charge? This book will present a lot of questions to help you find out, but you can start by answering these simple ones:

- ▶ Do I have enough money in the event that I get divorced or lose my spouse or significant other?
- ▶ Do I have enough money in the event that I become sick or disabled?
- ▶ Do I have enough money if I should lose my job or see my earnings drop?
- ▶ Do I have enough money if I should decide to start my own business?
- ▶ Do I have enough money if I want to retire?

▶ Do I know exactly how much money I have?

▶ Do I take good care of my money?

Don't worry if you answered "no" or "I'm not sure" to some, if not most, of these questions. The truth is, few women study their finances or save regularly, while women who actually have plenty of money don't know how to protect and grow their assets. But it doesn't have to be this way. And if you read on, maybe it won't be.

But before we even talk about money, it's important to get a sense of who you are and what you want. Not everyone hopes to make (or have) a million dollars, and not everyone wants to spend a lot of time thinking about money.

When I say I want you to have as much money as possible, I don't mean you should do so at the expense of what's important to you outside of money. I want you to have the best of both worlds—the spiritual and the material. Nourish your soul as well as your pocketbook. After all, money isn't everything. It isn't something to be worshiped. It *is* something to be valued, and to be accumulated, so that you have the freedom to live your life in accordance with your values.

If you have money to spare, I'm all in favor of giving it to charities that mean a lot to you. Just don't give to others in a way that harms you.

The following is a list of some nonmonetary values to consider. It provides a chance to think about what matters to you, and how that might impact your financial life. When you're ready to fill out your personal information worksheet on page 84, you'll need to keep in mind which activities you've checked off, particularly if you find, like most of us, that you're overspending and you need to cut back somewhere.

For instance, you may find that you're spending too much money in several areas, such as travel and entertainment. Yet you may realize that at the end of the day what really matters to you is your work at the church. Travel may come in a distant second, and entertainment you can do without until you have more to spend.

Or you may realize that your pets are your top priority, and you're willing to spend that extra money each month to make sure that Fifi and Koko are well cared for, even if it means selling your stamp collection.

I wish all of us could have everything we wanted. We can't. That's part of the human condition. But if you know your values, your desires, your dreams, you can at least work to surround yourself with what you want most.

So read this list carefully, and rate each item on a scale of 1–5, with 1 being least important and 5 being most important.

When you're done, see where the 5s are, and remember these high marks when it comes time to plan your financial life.

_____	Achievement	_____	Nature
_____	Aesthetics	_____	Pleasure
_____	Adventure	_____	Political Causes
_____	Animals	_____	Power
_____	Art	_____	Recreational Pursuits (Outdoor)
_____	Autonomy	_____	Recreational Pursuits (Indoor)
_____	Career	_____	Recognition
_____	Children	_____	Recovery
_____	Church/Church-related Activities	_____	Security
_____	Community Activities	_____	Service
_____	Continuing Education	_____	Sexuality
_____	Creativity	_____	Shopping (Don't laugh. For some, it's a reason to live.)
_____	Family	_____	Spirituality
_____	Friends	_____	Spontaneity
_____	Gardening	_____	Sports
_____	Health	_____	Technology
_____	Hobbies	_____	Travel
_____	Intimacy	_____	Volunteerism
_____	Love	_____	Wealth
_____	Money	_____	Wisdom

Now that you've considered your life's priorities and values, let's get down to another priority: your personal objectives. Do you have dreams? Do you have goals? Do you have desires (that can be fulfilled with money)? These, too, can be very helpful to bear in mind when trying to understand your finances, alone or with an advisor. Perhaps all you've ever wanted is a summer house, although you've never quite put that into words—but in order to get it, you're going to have to forgo vacations for a while. There are very few of us who can have everything we want, so think about what it is you want the most, and consider dropping what you want the least.

Goals

	Something I Truly Care About	Not Sure	Not Very Important
Eliminating debt			
Acquiring cash reserves	✓		
Retirement			
Minimizing taxes			
Long-term investments	✓		
Large savings account	✓		
Having/adopting children			
Children's education			
Grandchildren's education			
Children's wedding			
Minimizing estate tax			
Better health care			
Better insurance			
Providing for family in case of death			
Gifts to family			
Taking care of parents			

A new car	_____	_____	_____
The vacation of a lifetime	_____	_____	_____
A new house	✓_____	_____	_____
A summer home	_____	_____	_____
Career change	_____	_____	_____
Divorce	_____	_____	_____
Continuing education	_____	_____	_____
Gifts to charity	_____	_____	_____
Volunteerism	_____	_____	_____
Hobbies	_____	_____	_____
Other	_____	_____	_____
Other	_____	_____	_____
Other	_____	_____	_____
Other	_____	_____	_____
Other	_____	_____	_____

Okay. Now that you've thought about your values and your goals, you're ready to address your finances.

To do that, you're going to need access to your papers and records. Do you have that kind of ready access?

Frankly, very few women I meet do.

Manufacturers make files for a reason. People need them. So buy some. Take a pencil and mark on the top what's in it. This can be boring, I know. In my experience women just don't seem to like this kind of work. We hate files. We're used to writing on the backs of napkins in the kitchen. Well, it took a long time to get used to not having a tail when we evolved from monkeys. It takes a while to get used to everything. But you will get used to keeping good files. And remember not to throw anything away until you're sure you won't need it. Save your bank records, save your cancelled checks, save your policies—just as you're learning to save your money.

Personal Document Finder

Name _____

Address _____

Phone _____

Fax number _____

Person to call in case of emergency:

Name_____

Address _____

Phone _____

Social Sec. Numbers:

Mine _____   Husband _____

Child(ren)'s _____   _____

_____   _____

Others _____   _____

Treasury Bills, Notes, and Bonds

_____

_____

_____

_____

_____

Location _____

Tax-Free Bonds, Corporate Bonds

_____

_____

_____

_____

_____

Location _____

CDs

_____

_____

_____

_____

_____

Location _____

IRAs

_____

_____

_____

_____

_____

Location _____

Pension Funds

Type _____

Administrator _____

Phone _____

Trustee _____

Address _____

Insurance Policies

Life

Location _____

Name of co. _____

Type of policy _____

$ amount _____

Number _____

Agent _____

Address _____

Phone _____

Auto

Location _____

Name of co. _____

Type of policy _____

$ amount _____

Number _____

Agent _____

Address _____

Phone _____

Homeowner's

Location _____

Name of co. _____

Type of policy _____

$ amount _____

Number _____

Agent _____

Address _____

Phone _____

Liability

Location _____

Name of co. _____

Type of policy _____

$ amount _____

Number _____

Agent _____

Address _____

Phone _____

Health

Location _____

Name of co. _____

Type of policy _____

$ amount _____

Number _____

Agent _____

Address _____

Phone _____

Disability

Location _____

Name of co. _____

Type of policy _____

$ amount _____

Number _____

Agent _____

Address _____

Phone _____

Business

Location _____

Name of co. _____

Type of policy _____

$ amount _____

Number _____

Agent _____

Address _____

Phone _____

Malpractice

Location _____

Name of co. _____

Type of policy _____

$ amount _____

Number _____

Agent _____

Address _____

Phone _____

Other

Location _____

Name of co. _____

Type of policy _____

$ amount _____

Number _____

Agent _____

Address _____

Phone _____

Location of Important Papers

Auto title _____

Birth certificate _____

Passport _____

Death certificate _____

Marriage license _____

Divorce decree _____

Home deed _____

Loan agreements _____

Military records _____

Power of attorney _____

Religious information _____

Tax records _____

Will _____

Other _____

Jewelry

Location _____

Description _____

Appraised at $ _____

Safe Deposit Box

Location _____

Bank name _____

Address _____

Key location _____

Credit Cards

Co. name _____

№ _____

Co. name _____

№ _____

Co. name _____

№ _____

Co. name _____

№ _____

Co. name _____

№ _____

Co. name _____

№ _____

Important People and Phone Numbers

Accountant

Name_____

Address_____

Phone_____

Attorney ✓

Name_____

Address_____

Phone_____

Bank (er) ✓

Name_____

Address_____

Phone_____

Broker ✓

Name_____

Address_____

Phone_____

Children

Name_____

Address_____

Phone_____

Name_____

Address_____

Phone_____

Name_____

Address_____

Phone_____

Clergy

Name _____

Address _____

Phone _____

Company Personnel Office

Name _____

Address _____

Phone _____

Doctor

Name _____

Address _____

Phone _____

Emergency Room

Address _____

Phone _____

Executor

Name _____

Address _____

Phone _____

Financial Planner/Money Manager, etc.

Name _____

Address _____

Phone _____

Parents

Name _____

Address _____

Phone _____

Keeping Track of Your Stocks

First, use this form to list all your stocks. (If you have a broker, you won't actually possess the stock certificates.)

Broker (if applicable) _____

Broker account number _____

Company	Certificate Shares Number	Date Issued	Location

Now use this form to follow your stocks. You don't need to do this every day. You're in for the long haul, remember? Once a month will probably be sufficient.

Company	Nº of Shares	Date Bought	Cost	Div Recvd	Stock Div.	Stock Split	Date of Div. or Split	Date Sold	Sales Price

Company	Nº of Shares	Date Bought	Cost	Div Recvd	Stock Div.	Stock Split	Date of Div. or Split	Date Sold	Sales Price
_____	_____	_____	_____	_____	_____	_____	_____	_____	_____
_____	_____	_____	_____	_____	_____	_____	_____	_____	_____
_____	_____	_____	_____	_____	_____	_____	_____	_____	_____
_____	_____	_____	_____	_____	_____	_____	_____	_____	_____
_____	_____	_____	_____	_____	_____	_____	_____	_____	_____
_____	_____	_____	_____	_____	_____	_____	_____	_____	_____
_____	_____	_____	_____	_____	_____	_____	_____	_____	_____
_____	_____	_____	_____	_____	_____	_____	_____	_____	_____
_____	_____	_____	_____	_____	_____	_____	_____	_____	_____
_____	_____	_____	_____	_____	_____	_____	_____	_____	_____
_____	_____	_____	_____	_____	_____	_____	_____	_____	_____

Keeping Track of Your Bonds

Company	Type of Bond	Issue Date	Interest	Certificate Number	Maturity Date
_____	_____	_____	_____	_____	_____
_____	_____	_____	_____	_____	_____
_____	_____	_____	_____	_____	_____
_____	_____	_____	_____	_____	_____
_____	_____	_____	_____	_____	_____
_____	_____	_____	_____	_____	_____
_____	_____	_____	_____	_____	_____

Okay. Your next step is to fill out the information worksheet.

When you do, be honest. Only you will see your results. Still, you'd be surprised how many people just don't want to face up to the truth. Lord knows I've run into many women—and many men, too—who haven't been able to fill out a fact sheet without resorting to fiction. Sure, they say, I know what I make, I know what I spend, I know what comes in and out of my wallet. Wrong. They're in denial. And the only way they can continue pretending they're not is to avoid filling out these kinds of forms so they never write down what they have, how much they spend, and how much they have left.

So please, please, please, please, be honest.

You don't have to fill out every line, by the way. Much of it won't apply to you—just put down the information that's pertinent.

Confidential Information Worksheet

Personal Information

Date _____

Client name(s) and age(s)_____

Address _____

Phone numbers:

    Business _____ Home _____

Occupation:

    Self _____ Spouse _____

Family Information

Enter your dependents' names and dates of birth:

Name   Birth date (or age)

_____   _____

_____   _____

_____   _____

_____   _____

What do you want to accomplish from this financial consultation and future planning?

_____

_____

_____

Do you have any short-term goals, e.g., buying a new home or boat, that would be relevant to your financial planning?

_____

_____

_____

Financial Independence

At what age do you plan to be financially independent?   _____

At what age would you ideally like to retire?   _____

How much monthly income is needed to retire comfortably?   _____

                                                                                    (in today's economy?)

How much have you invested to date for retirement?   _____

How much will your company retirement plan pay?   _____

What plans have you made to date about retirement?

_____

_____

Estate Planning Information

In the event of your death, how much annual income is needed for your family:

Until your youngest child is out of high school? _____

For your spouse after the children are grown? _____

Amount saved for your children's education? _____

Cost annually for each child's undergraduate study? _____

Cost annually for graduate studies? _____

I have (a) plan(s) for my practice/business at death   Y _____ N _____ N/A _____

Do both spouses have a will/trust?   Y _____ N _____

Life and Disability Insurance Benefits

What is the face amount of your life insurance? _____

What is the amount of insurance on your spouse? _____

Amount of insurance provided by your company? _____

Disability benefits at work or from a personal policy? _____

How much? _____

How much in liquid emergency funds are needed? _____

Financial Assets and Debts

(Attach copy of recent statement showing details where applicable)

	Value	Market Annual Rate of Return/ Growth Rate
Personal Liquid Assets		
Checking accounts	$ _____	_____ %
Certificates of deposit	$ _____	_____ %

	Value	Market Annual Rate of Return/ Growth Rate
Stocks	$ _____	_____ %
Bonds—taxable	$ _____	_____ %
Bonds—tax-free	$ _____	_____ %
Mutual funds	$ _____	_____ %
Other	$ _____	_____ %
Other	$ _____	_____ %
Other	$ _____	_____ %

Retirement Plan Assets

	Value	
IRA accounts	$ _____	_____ %
Self-employed plan	$ _____	_____ %
Company retirement plans	$ _____	_____ %
Other	$ _____	_____ %

Real Estate

	Value	Mortgage Balance
Residence	$ _____	_____
Vacation/second residence	$ _____	_____
Rental	$ _____	_____

Business or Practice Value

	Value
_____ _____	$ _____
_____ _____	$ _____

Debts

	Unpaid Balance
Investment loans (other than real estate)	$ _____
Consumer debts (autos, charge accounts, etc.)	$ _____

Now, if we were sitting down at a planning session together, we'd look over your worksheet, and study your assets as well as your debts.

Indeed, what are your assets? Your retirement plan assets? Real estate? Business or professional practice value? What about your debts? If you have both credit-card debt and savings, then simply deduct that debt from your savings. Credit-card debt is one debt you must get rid of. Why? Because you're paying a ridiculous premium for it—more than you could ever earn through a normal investment vehicle. Once this subtraction has been done, you may notice you have zero savings. Your first job is to get some!

Now look at how much you earn per month and per year. That figure is your total income (line C).

Then, on line F, add up your personal expenses. Next on the agenda are your business/investment expenses, if applicable.

Add these two sets of expenses. Your total income minus your total expenses is what you have left to save.

Next, fill out the Personal Treadmill Statement of Cash Flow that starts on page 90. As named by my accountant Joel Framson, these are expenses that keep coming up and up and up, no matter what you do. This page will give you an idea of what you're spending, and when you're spending it.

Remember—be honest. Everything you spend counts. Everything. What you lay out for clothes, for food, for shelter, even for electricity. If we've left off any items, please add them to the list.

I look particularly closely at those expenses that we like to think are nonrecurring. Ever notice how something manages to happen that makes them recur again anyway? That vacation to Europe—you say it's a one-time thing, but why, when we look at your spending patterns over the last few years, are there vacations listed every year? Oh, you say, those vacations weren't to Europe. Those were elsewhere. Yes, women have told me that, as if to say, that's not an expense that counts, that's just a one-time splurge. A one-time splurge every year, as it turns out.

On page 94 we give you a chance to reduce those treadmill expenses. Write down in column A what you now spend on these items.

Next write down in column B what you would spend if you were willing to save just a little.

Now take that one step further, and really squeeze. Do you truly need that new dress every month? Or every year?

Correcting Your Credit Report

It can happen to anyone. You've always paid your bills, you've never stiffed a soul. Then one day you go in to buy a car and the salesman runs your name through a computer and looks at you as though you were a felon.

Why? Because mistakes happen. Even if you have a great credit background, you may find that somehow, some way, someone misreported your history, a computer made an error, or your name was just too similar to that of some woman with the worst credit rating on earth.

You can do something about it. You can write to any of these three companies and get a copy of your credit report to make sure that it's accurate:

Equifax	TRW	Trans Union Corp.
P.O. Box 105873	P.O. Box 8030	P.O. Box 390
Atlanta, GA 30348	Layton, UT 84041	Springfield PA 19064
(800) 685-1111	(800) 392-1122	(440) 779-7200

Then fill out the last column with your adjusted budget numbers, based on the best you think you can do on reducing these expenses.

What's the bottom line?

Let me put it gently: If you don't save, you may face ruin some day. You'll have an emergency and you won't be able to do anything about it. You'll be at the mercy of the system, your parents, your husband, or your ex-husband. Or you'll be pushing a shopping cart down Main Street. So don't save for my sake. Save for yours. You want to have choices in life. You want to have freedom. That's the greatest gift savings provide you.

So maybe that wasn't gentle. But it was the truth.

Now, if you can figure out a way to make more money, terrific. Turn on that switch. But most people can't. So instead you must, must, must start saving. Where do you begin? Cut back on the least necessary things, like those outfits you never wear, or the Caribbean vacations, or traveling first class when coach would do just fine.

This advice doesn't apply to everyone. There are some people who don't have to change anything. They are organized, effective managers of their own money. Good for them. I once had a wealthy client whom I actually told to go out and spend more money. What was she saving it for? I wondered. Be nice to yourself, I told her, you can afford almost anything.

Still, in all the years I've been working, I've only met one such person.

Personal Treadmill
Statement of Cash Flow

For the year ended December 31, _____

Personal Income	**Monthly Estimate**	**Annual Estimate**
Salary, wages, tips	_____	_____
Pension retirement income	_____	_____
Social security	_____	_____
Other personal income	_____	_____
Total personal income (A)	_____	_____

Business/Investment Income		
Business income	_____	_____
Rent/royalty income	_____	_____
Interest/dividend income	_____	_____
Other investment income	_____	_____
Total bus./inv. income (B)	_____	_____
Total Income (A + B = C)	_____	_____

Personal Expenses

	Monthly Estimate	Annual Estimate
Living expenses (*from next page*)	_____	_____
Personal income taxes	_____	_____
Social-security taxes	_____	_____
Education expenses	_____	_____
Personal-debt service:		
Mortgage principal and interest	_____	_____
Other interest	_____	_____
Other expenses	_____	_____
Total personal expenses (D)	_____	_____

Business/Investment Expenses

Business/investment income taxes	_____	_____
Investment-debt service:		
Principal	_____	_____
Interest	_____	_____
Other bus./inv. expenses	_____	_____
Total bus./inv. expenses (E)	_____	_____
Total Expenses (D + E = F)	_____	_____
Cash available for long-term uses (C-F)	_____	_____

Treadmill Living Expenses

Recreation

	Monthly Estimate	Annual Estimate
Dining out		
Movies		
Recreation		
Vacations		
Hobbies		
Country club		
Summer camp		
Sporting events		
Entertaining		

Transportation

Auto lease		
Gasoline		
Public transportation		
Parking & tolls		
Maintenance/repairs		
License plates & fees		

Household

Rent		
Condo/assoc. fees		
Gas & electricity		
Telephone		
Household maintenance		
Water & sewage		
Groceries		

	Monthly Estimate	Annual Estimate
Child care		
Clothing		
Lawn care		

Gifts

	Monthly Estimate	Annual Estimate
Birthdays		
Holidays		
Anniversaries		
Special occasions		

Miscellaneous

	Monthly Estimate	Annual Estimate
Barber/beauty parlor		
Dry cleaning		
Newspapers/subscriptions		
Pet care		
Domestic help		
Allowances		
Adult care		
Lessons		
Cosmetics & personal care		
Other		

Itemized Deductions

	Monthly Estimate	Annual Estimate
Medicine & medical bills		
Property taxes		
Cash charitable contributions		
Other itemized deductions		

Insurance Premiums

	Monthly Estimate	Annual Estimate
Auto	_____	_____
Homeowners	_____	_____
Disability	_____	_____
Health	_____	_____
Life	_____	_____
Personal liability	_____	_____
Other insurance	_____	_____
Total Living Expenses	_____	_____

Adjusted Treadmill Living Expenses

For those looking to hold down expenses, we use this list to help you figure out where you can cut back. First put down under column A what you spend on each item (from the Annual Estimate column above). Then, in column B, write down what you think you could spend if you were willing to save a little. If this gets you to where you'd like to be in terms of budget, then you can stop. Otherwise, try again with column C, saving still a little more. Then write down your adjusted total on the final line.

Recreation

	A List	B List	C List	Adj. Total
Dining out	_____	_____	_____	_____
Movies	_____	_____	_____	_____
Recreation	_____	_____	_____	_____
Vacations	_____	_____	_____	_____
Hobbies	_____	_____	_____	_____
Country club	_____	_____	_____	_____
Summer camp	_____	_____	_____	_____

	A List	B List	C List	Adj. Total
Sporting events				
Entertaining				

Transportation

Auto lease				
Gasoline				
Public transportation				
Parking & tolls				
Maintenance/repairs				
License plates & fees				

Household

Rent				
Condo/assoc. fees				
Gas & electricity				
Telephone				
Household maintenance				
Water & sewage				
Groceries				
Child care				
Clothing				
Lawn care				

Gifts

Birthdays				
Holidays				
Anniversaries				
Special occasions				

Miscellaneous

	A List	B List	C List	Adj. Total
Barber/beauty parlor				
Dry cleaning				
Newspapers/subscriptions				
Pet care				
Domestic help				
Allowances				
Adult care				
Lessons				
Cosmetics & personal care				
Other				

Itemized Deductions

	A List	B List	C List	Adj. Total
Medicine & medical bills				
Property taxes				
Cash charitable contr'ns				
Other itemized deductions				

Insurance Premiums

	A List	B List	C List	Adj. Total
Auto				
Homeowners				
Disability				
Health				
Life				
Person Liability				
Other Insurance				

Total Adjusted Treadmill Living Expenses

Now you know how much you have, how much you spend, and how much you earn. Let's talk about a few other important issues. Investing your money is critical, but before you can do that, you need to make sure that you've taken care of some other essential parts of your financial well-being: your retirement fund, your estate planning, and your insurance needs.

Retirement

Pity us women! We're in much worse shape than men when it comes to retirement. Three out of five women who work in the private sector don't have a pension plan. Furthermore, women have less discretionary income available for savings, since they earn 72 cents for every dollar a man makes. And women change jobs more often than men—every 5.8 years, versus 7.6 for men—meaning that we're less likely to become vested in our company pension plans even if we have them. As of now, 55 percent of men over the age of 55 receive some pension benefits, as opposed to only 32 percent of women.

So let's get going and start planning. You should know *now* how much money you'll need the day you walk away from your job and face whatever wonderful projects you've planned for the rest of your life.

In order to calculate the amount of money you'll need for retirement, figure out what your current needs are—how much you spend, where you spend it—and then project that into the future by factoring in inflation as shown here.

Inflation Multiplier

If you want to figure out how inflation will affect the future cost of expected expenditures, use this table: Multiply the item's present cost by the multiplier below, depending on the number of years in the future you're thinking about and the anticipated percentage inflation.

In other words, if you're thinking about spending $20,000 two years from now on a big-ticket item whose price keeps up with inflation, and the inflation rate for those two years is expected to be 4-percent each year, then multiply the $20,000 by 1.08, and the new cost in two years will be $21,600.

(continued)

Years in Future	2%	4%	6%	8%	10%	12%
1	1.02	1.04	1.06	1.08	1.10	1.12
2	1.04	1.08	1.12	1.17	1.21	1.25
3	1.06	1.12	1.19	1.26	1.33	1.40
4	1.08	1.17	1.26	1.36	1.46	1.57
5	1.10	1.22	1.34	1.47	1.61	1.76
6	1.12	1.27	1.42	1.59	1.77	1.97
7	1.14	1.32	1.50	1.71	1.95	2.21
8	1.16	1.37	1.59	1.85	2.14	2.48
9	1.18	1.42	1.69	2.00	2.36	2.77
10	1.20	1.48	1.79	2.16	2.59	3.11
15	1.33	1.80	2.40	3.17	4.18	5.47
20	1.48	2.19	3.21	4.66	6.73	9.65
25	1.63	2.67	4.29	6.85	10.83	17.00

So today you're getting by on $50,000 a year. But you know about that bugaboo called inflation, that terrible scourge that comes and eats away at the value of your money every year.

Inflation is a guaranteed factor in your future—but how much is it going to be? Not that long ago we were all getting used to double digit inflation. Then we got used to low inflation. So no one knows what inflation will do to your dollar, but you still need to think ahead, knowing that your $50,000 this year isn't going to be worth that in twenty years. This chart can give you a sense of how much you'll need to save to match that $50,000. For instance, if you think that the next twenty-five years will average 12 percent inflation, multiply that 50,000 by 17, and you get 425,000. $425,000! Better start saving right now!

The standard calculation that most experts seem to feel works best is the following: When you retire, you can get by on 75 percent of your current income, since your needs tend to lessen. For instance, if you have kids, by the time you retire, you'll no longer be supporting them (I hope); if you have a mortgage, you probably will have paid it off by that time, and so on.

Here's one way to figure out how much you'll need (remember, you don't have to worry about whether these figures are exact. Just do your best):

1. Annual income requirement (75% of today's requirement) _____

2. Annual income requirement factoring in inflation
   (see pages 97 and 98) _____

3. Annual amount received from pensions, etc. _____

4. Annual social security benefit _____

5. Other retirement income _____

6. Total retirement income (sum of lines 3, 4, and 5) _____

Now look at the difference between lines 2 and 6. If 6 is smaller than 2 (and for most people it will be), you'll need to supplement your retirement income with returns from savings and whatever else goes into your retirement fund.

Here's something of consequence to keep in mind when thinking about these figures: You're never too young to start saving. Never.

There are two fundamental aspects of a retirement savings program. The first is time: Nothing beats time for investing. A thousand dollars set aside in a tax-free account for twenty years at 10 percent interest will grow to $6,727. In forty years, it will grow to $45,259. And if you're able to hold it for sixty years, you'll have earned more than $300,000 on that original $1,000. Over time, nothing beats time. It's the best friend an investor ever had.

Quick. Let's say you have two options. One is to invest $75 every month at an average rate of 8.5 percent a year. The other is to wait 10 years, and then invest $200 a month—or a little more than two and a half times 75. At the end of 20 years, which plan will earn you more money?

In the first instance, you've invested only $18,000, and in the second you've put in $24,000. But the first plan will net you $47,358, while the second plan will give you only $37,894. That's a difference of almost $10,000 achieved simply by giving your money more time to grow.

The way money grows is by compounding, which refers to the way interest is earned on the principal amount and is then reinvested. Every time interest is earned, it's added to the principal, so the base amount grows. Earning interest on an ever-increasing amount accelerates its growth.

Tax-free compounding over years is the reason time will work so well for you, for if the $1,000 mentioned earlier had been taxed over those sixty years, you'd have considerably less money.

Here's what happens if you put $100 a month aside for anywhere between one and forty years, at various rates of return from 5 to 10 percent, before taxes. For example, if you were to put $100 into a CD at 5 percent interest, after forty years you'd have $153,238. Nice work, if you can get it. And you can!

	1	2	3	4	5	10	15	20	25	30	35	40
5.00%	$1,233	$2,529	$3,891	$5,324	$6,829	$15,593	$26,840	$41,275	$59,799	$83,573	$114,083	$153,238
5.25%	$1,235	$2,536	$3,907	$5,352	$6,874	$15,807	$27,414	$42,496	$62,095	$87,563	$120,656	$163,658
5.50%	$1,236	$2,542	$3,922	$5,380	$6,920	$16,024	$28,002	$43,762	$64,498	$91,780	$127,675	$174,902
5.75%	$1,238	$2,549	$3,938	$5,408	$6,966	$16,245	$28,607	$45,075	$67,013	$96,239	$135,172	$187,039
6.00%	$1,240	$2,556	$3,953	$5,437	$7,012	$16,470	$29,227	$46,435	$69,646	$100,954	$143,183	$200,145
6.25%	$1,241	$2,563	$3,969	$5,466	$7,059	$16,699	$29,865	$47,845	$72,403	$105,941	$151,745	$214,302
6.50%	$1,243	$2,569	$3,985	$5,495	$7,106	$16,932	$30,519	$49,308	$75,289	$111,217	$160,898	$229,599
6.75%	$1,245	$2,576	$4,000	$5,524	$7,153	$17,168	$31,191	$50,824	$78,313	$116,800	$170,686	$246,134
7.00%	$1,246	$2,583	$4,016	$5,553	$7,201	$17,409	$31,881	$52,397	$81,480	$122,709	$181,156	$264,012
7.25%	$1,248	$2,590	$4,032	$5,583	$7,249	$17,655	$32,590	$54,027	$84,798	$128,964	$192,358	$283,350
7.50%	$1,250	$2,597	$4,048	$5,612	$7,298	$17,904	$33,318	$55,719	$88,274	$135,587	$204,345	$304,272
7.75%	$1,252	$2,604	$4,064	$5,642	$7,347	$18,158	$34,066	$57,474	$91,918	$142,600	$217,178	$326,915
8.00%	$1,253	$2,611	$4,081	$5,673	$7,397	$18,417	$34,835	$59,295	$95,737	$150,030	$230,918	$351,428
8.25%	$1,255	$2,618	$4,097	$5,703	$7,447	$18,680	$35,624	$61,184	$99,740	$157,900	$245,632	$377,973
8.50%	$1,257	$2,625	$4,113	$5,733	$7,497	$18,947	$36,435	$63,144	$103,937	$166,240	$261,395	$406,726
8.75%	$1,258	$2,631	$4,130	$5,764	$7,548	$19,219	$37,268	$65,178	$108,338	$175,078	$278,284	$437,880
9.00%	$1,260	$2,638	$4,146	$5,795	$7,599	$19,497	$38,124	$67,290	$112,953	$184,447	$296,385	$471,643

	1	2	3	4	5	10	15	20	25	30	35	40
9.25%	$1.262	$2.646	$4.163	$5.826	$7.651	$19.779	$39.004	$69.481	$117.794	$194.380	$315.787	$508.245
9.50%	$1.264	$2.653	$4.179	$5.858	$7.703	$20.066	$39.908	$71.756	$122.872	$204.913	$336.590	$547.933
9.75%	$1.265	$2.660	$4.196	$5.889	$7.755	$20.358	$40.837	$74.118	$128.199	$216.084	$358.899	$590.979
10.00%	$1.267	$2.667	$4.213	$5.921	$7.808	$20.655	$41.792	$76.570	$133.789	$227.933	$382.828	$637.678

The second fundamental aspect of savings is discipline. Saving doesn't come easily to most people. But the sooner you learn how to do it, the better off you'll be. Regularly paying yourself a certain amount of money every month is the surest way to guarantee having a savings account. Save money each and every month. Pay yourself X percent of your salary. Then, at the end of the month, if you have money left over, put that into your investment portfolio, too.

Unfortunately, you can't depend on social security. It may not be around by the time you retire. And even if it is, social security doesn't constitute a full retirement program—its benefits are too low. When the system was designed, social security paid small but reasonable benefits. However, inflation has taken care of that over the years.

These days, all the other retirement savings plans you've heard about take the place of social security: 401(k), 403(b), IRAs (Individual Retirement Accounts), Roth IRAs, Keoghs, SEPs (simplified employee pensions), pension plans, etc. All of these plans offer you ways to grow your money tax free. Any time the government offers you a way to make money without taxation, jump on it.

The IRS has a hot line for anyone interested in these plans: (800) 829-3676. You can also call the American Association of Retired Persons (AARP): (202) 434-2277.

Taxes

Now let's talk about taxes.

Everyone pays taxes. If you don't, you go to jail. End of story.

How best to plan for taxes? The bottom line: Don't spend the part of your income that's going to be taxed. If you have a full-time job, your employer deducts taxes every week, so there shouldn't be any surprises at the end of the year. And if you're self-employed, you should be paying taxes quarterly, so pay attention to what's coming up every April, June, September, and January. Seems obvious, no?

And yet I've found that, much more often than men, women fail to focus on the taxable part of their income when preparing their budgets. They often think more in terms of *gross* income rather than *net* (gross is your money before you've paid taxes, and net is what's left afterward).

The most important step you can take is finding a good tax adviser to help you. Unless you're able to use the short form knowledgeably, or you're that singular person who understands tax rules, consider hiring an expert. More than half the country does.

The tax laws are not only complicated, they are continuously changing. The person you choose to prepare your taxes should be someone who stays well informed of tax developments. At the very least she should be educated as an accountant or should be an "enrolled agent" (someone who's been certified by the IRS to prepare taxes) with several years' experience.

And don't look for a tax adviser based on how little tax she claims she can "arrange" for you. Similarly, when you first meet with a new adviser, make sure she doesn't wink and insinuate about the "funny" things she might be able to do. If you don't think she's on the level, leave. Because when completing your tax returns, the cardinal, primary, principal, elemental, fundamental, ultimate rule is: Be honest.

And be ready when it's tax time. One of the silliest ways to waste money is to hire a tax adviser at $100 an hour and then spend the first seven hours of his time getting him to organize your records. Be prepared. Fill out a form like the following *before* you go into the preparer's office:

Tax Time Tips:

► Don't forget that alimony is taxable (and tax deductible for those that pay it)—but child support is not.
► If the tax preparation fees in your area are too high, try one of the national storefront chains, such as H&R Block, or Beneficial Income Tax Service. They're very reasonable—the average fee is around $60.

- Be prepared. Even if you're not currently involved in your own financial affairs, you still must organize your own papers. Keep track of everything, such as your will, your husband's will, any trusts you or he own, insurance policies, etc. When you visit your tax preparer, you'll save time if you bring in everything you need.

- If you know that you're owed a refund, file early. You'll get your refund earlier. Who would you rather have earning interest income, the government or you?

- Coordinate your tax planning with estate planning, investment planning, and retirement planning. All these areas work together: If you plan badly in one area, all the others will be affected.

- If you need to, you can extend the deadline for filing your return. But be sure you fill out the correct forms. Ask your tax preparer for help.

- If you prepare your own taxes and own a computer, there's some excellent software out there to help. Try TurboTax or MacIntax.

- Pay your mortgage on time, or even a month early in order to receive an extra month's interest expense deduction.

- If you do free-lance work at home, ask your preparer to see if you qualify for a home-office deduction. The IRS has stiffened these rules, but it's always worth checking.

- Don't forget that an individual is permitted to give someone up to $10,000 each year without paying taxes on it. For instance, a couple can give a total of $20,000 to each child. This rule can help you save on estate taxes.

- The IRS publishes dozens of pamphlets to help you understand their rules and your obligations. You can order them at (800) TAX-FORM (829-3676). They also have a Web site: http://www.irs.ustreas.gov/basic/cover/html.

- Want more information from the IRS? Use their TeleTax recorded Tax and Refund Information Line: TeleTax 1-800 Numbers

- If you need still more information, try the IRS's 1-800 Tax Assistance Telephone Numbers:

Tax Help Telephone Numbers

Alabama	(800) 829-1040	New York	BUFFALO: (716) 685-5432
Alaska	(800) 829-1040		ELSEWHERE: (800) 829-1040
Arizona	(800) 829-1040	North Carolina	(800) 829-1040
Arkansas	(800) 829-1040	North Dakota	(800) 829-1040
California	OAKLAND: (510) 839-1040	Ohio	CINCINNATI:
	ELSEWHERE: (800) 829-1040		(513) 621-6281
Colorado	DENVER: (303) 825-7041		CLEVELAND: (216) 522-3000
	ELSEWHERE: (800) 829-1040		ELSEWHERE: (800) 829-1040
Connecticut	(800) 829-1040	Oklahoma	(800) 829-1040
Delaware	(800) 829-1040	Oregon	PORTLAND: (503) 221-3960
D.C.	(800) 829-1040		ELSEWHERE: (800) 829-1040
Florida	JACKSONVILLE:	Pennsylvania	PHILADELPHIA:
	(904) 354-1760		(215) 574-9900
	ELSEWHERE: (800) 829-1040		PITTSBURGH:
Hawaii	(800) 829-1040		(412) 281-0112
Idaho	(800) 829-1040		ELSEWHERE: (800) 829-1040
Illinois	(800) 829-1040	Puerto Rico	SAN JUAN METRO AREA:
Indiana	(800) 829-1040		(878) 759-5100
Iowa	(800) 829-1040		ELSEWHERE: (800) 829-1040
Kansas	(800) 829-1040	Rhode Island	(800) 829-1040
Kentucky	(800) 829-1040	South Carolina	(800) 829-1040
Lousiana	(800) 829-1040	South Dakota	(800) 829-1040
Maine	(800) 829-1040	Tennessee	NASHVILLE: (615) 834-9005
Maryland	BALTIMORE: (410) 962-2590		ELSEWHERE: (800) 829-1040
	ELSEWHERE: (800) 829-1040	Texas	DALLAS: (214) 742-2440
Massachusetts	BOSTON: (617) 536-1041		HOUSTON: (713) 541-0440
	ELSEWHERE: (800) 829-1040		ELSEWHERE:
Michigan	(800) 829-1040		(800) 829-1040
Minnesota	(800) 829-1040	Utah	(800) 829-1040
Mississippi	(800) 829-1040	Vermont	(800) 829-1040
Missouri	ST. LOUIS: (314) 342-1040	Virginia	RICHMOND:
	ELSEWHERE: (800) 829-1040		(804) 698-5000
Montana	(800) 829-1040		ELSEWHERE:
Nebraska	(800) 829-1040		(800) 829-1040
Nevada	(800) 829-1040	Washington	SEATTLE: (206) 442-1040
New Hampshire			ELSEWHERE: (800) 829-1040
	(800) 829-1040	West Virginia	(800) 829-1040
New Jersey	(800) 829-1040	Wisconsin	(800) 829-1040
New Mexico	(800) 829-1040	Wyoming	(800) 829-1040

And finally, if you've filled out your taxes but lost your pre-addressed envelope, here's where to send your return:

Mailing Address of Internal Revenue Service Centers

If an envelope addressed to the Internal Revenue Service center came with your tax booklet, and you are filing a paper return, please use it. If you do not have one, or if you moved during the year, mail you return to the Internal Revenue Service Center indicated for your state. A street address is not needed.

Alabama	Memphis, TN 37501	**Kansas**	Austin, TX 73301
Alaska	Ogden, UT 84201	**Kentucky**	Cincinnati, OH 45999
Arizona	Ogden, UT 84201	**Louisiana**	Memphis, TN 37501
Arkansas	Memphis, TN 37501	**Maine**	Andover, MA 05501
California		**Maryland**	Philadelphia, PA 19255

California

COUNTIES OF ALPINE, AMADOR, BUTTE, CALAVERAS, COLUSA, CONTRA COSTA, DEL NORTE, EL DORADO, GLENN, HUMBOLDT, LAKE, LASSEN, MARIN, MENDOCINO, MODOC, NAPA, NEVADA, PLACER, PLUMAS, SACRAMENTO, SAN JOAQUIN, SHASTA, SIERRA, SISKIYOU, SOLANO, SONOMA, SUTTER, TEHAMA, TRINITY, YOLO, AND YUBA

    Ogden, UT 84201

ALL OTHER COUNTIES

    Fresno, CA 93888

Colorado Ogden, UT 84201

Connecticut Andover, MA 05501

Delaware Philadelphia, PA 19255

District of Columbia

    Philadelphia, PA 19255

Florida Atlanta, GA 39901

Georgia Atlanta, GA 39901

Hawaii Fresno, CA 93888

Idaho Ogden, UT 84201

Illinois Kansas City, MO 64999

Indiana Cincinnati, OH 45999

Iowa Kansas City, MO 64999

Kansas Austin, TX 73301

Kentucky Cincinnati, OH 45999

Louisiana Memphis, TN 37501

Maine Andover, MA 05501

Maryland Philadelphia, PA 19255

Massachusetts Andover, MA 05501

Michigan Cincinnati, OH 45999

Minnesota Kanas City, MO 64999

Mississippi Memphis, TN 37501

Missouri Kansas City, MO 64999

Montana Ogden, UT 84201

Nebraska Ogden, UT 84201

Nevada Ogden, UT 84201

New Hampshire

    Andover, MA 05501

New Jersey Holtsville, NY 00501

New Mexico Austin, TX 73301

New York

NEW YORK CITY AND COUNTIES OF NASSAU, ROCKLAND, SUFFOLK, AND WESTCHESTER

    Holtsville, NY 00501

ALL OTHER COUNTIES

    Andover, MA 05501

North Carolina

    Memphis, TN 37501

North Dakota Ogden, UT 84201

Ohio Cincinnati, OH 45999

Oklahoma Austin, TX 73301

Oregon	Ogden, UT 84201
Pennsylvania	Philadelphia, PA 19255
Rhode Island	Andover, MA 05501
South Carolina	
	Atlanta, GA 39901
South Dakota	Ogden, UT 84201
Tennessee	Memphis, TN 37501
Texas	Austin, TX 73301
Utah	Ogden, UT 84201
Vermont	Andover, MA 05501
Virginia	Philadelphia, PA 19255
Washington	Ogden, UT 84201
West Virginia	Cincinnati, OH 45999
Wisconsin	Kansas City, MO 64999
Wyoming	Ogden, UT 84201
American Samoa	
	Philadelphia, PA 19255

Guam

PERMANENT RESIDENTS:

Department of Revenue
and Taxation

Government of Guam
P.O. Box 23607
GMF, GU 96921

NONPERMANENT RESIDENTS:

Philadelphia, PA 19255

Puerto Rico Philadelphia, PA 19255

Virgin Islands

PERMANENT RESIDENTS:

V.I. Bureau of Internal
Revenue
9601 Estate Thomas
Charlotte Amalie
St. Thomas, VI 00802

NONPERMANENT RESIDENTS:

Philadelphia, PA 19255

Foreign Country

U.S. CITIZENS AND THOSE FILING FORM
2555, FORM 2555-EZ, OR FORM 4563
Philadelphia, PA 19255

All APO and FPO addresses
Philadelphia, PA 19255

Now, if you do want to surprise your tax helper with advance work, or if you just are curious how much you're going to owe, you're welcome to fill out the following form.

Tax Planning Worksheet

Gross Income:	Last Year	This Year
Taxable wages/salaries	_____	_____
Taxable dividends/interest	_____	_____
Net business income (or loss)	_____	_____
Net taxable long-term capital gain (or loss)	_____	_____

	Last Year	This Year
Net taxable short-term capital gain (or loss)	_____	_____
Net rent income (or loss)	_____	_____
Net partnership income (or loss)	_____	_____
Other income	_____	_____

Adjustments to Gross Income:

	Last Year	This Year
Alimony	_____	_____
IRA/SEP payments	_____	_____
Keogh plan payments	_____	_____
Unreimbursed business expenses	_____	_____
Deduction for working married couple	_____	_____
Other adjustments	_____	_____
Adjusted Gross Income	_____	_____

Itemized Deductions:

	Last Year	This Year
Medical	_____	_____
Taxes	_____	_____
Interest paid	_____	_____
Gifts to charity	_____	_____
Accident/theft/fire loss	_____	_____
Other	_____	_____
Total Itemized Deductions	_____	_____
Standard Deduction	_____	_____
Exemptions _____ at $ _____ each	_____	_____
Taxable Income	_____	_____
Tax	_____	_____
Withholding	_____	_____

Federal Estimated Payments:

April _____ _____

June _____ _____

Sept. _____ _____

Jan. _____ _____

And, in case you want to know how much your taxes are in advance, here are the 1998 rate schedules:

1998 Tax Rate Schedules

1998 - Single - Schedule X

If your taxable income is:

Over	But not over	Your tax is:	of the amount over
$0	$25,350	15%	$0
25,350	61,400	$3,802.50 × 28%	25,350
61,400	128,100	13,802.50 × 31%	61,400
128,100	278,450	39,770.00 × 36%	128,100
278,450	—	88,870.00 × 39.6%	278,450

1998 - Married Filing Jointly or Qualifying Widow(er) - Schedule Y-1

If your taxable income is:

Over	But not over	The tax is:	of the amount over
$0	$42,350	15%	$0
42,350	102,300	$3,802.50 × 28%	42,350
102,300	155,950	23,138.50 × 31%	102,300
155,950	278,450	39,770.00 × 36%	155,950
278,450	—	88,870.00 × 39.6%	278,450

1998 - Married Filing Separately or Qualifying Widow(er) - Schedule Y-2

If your taxable income is:

Over	But not over	The tax is:	of the amount over
$0	$21,175	15%	$0
21,175	51,150	$3,176.25×28%	21,175
51,150	77,975	11,569.25×31%	51,150
77,975	139,225	19,885.00×36%	77,975
139,225	—	41,935.00×39.6%	139,225

1998 - Head of Household - Schedule Z

If your taxable income is:

Over	But not over	The tax is:	of the amount over
$0	$33,950	15%	$0
33,950	87,700	$5,092.50×28%	33,950
87,700	142,000	20,142.50×31%	87,700
142,000	278,450	36,975.50×36%	142,000
278,450		86,097.50×39.6%	278,450

Tax Publications

The IRS produces many free publications to help you fill out your tax return and to answer your tax questions.

All IRS publications and forms can be downloaded from the Internet or ordered at no charge by calling the IRS at 1-800-829-3676. You can also get forms faxed to you.

Tax Publications and Related Forms

You may want to get one or more of the publications listed below for information on a specific topic. Where the publication title may not be enough to describe the contents of the publication, there is a brief description. Forms and schedules related to the contents of each publication are shown after each listing.

Popular Publications

Pub 17, Your Federal Income Tax (For Individuals)—can help you prepare your individual tax return. This publication takes you step-by-step through each part of the return. It explains the tax laws in a way that will help you better understand your taxes so that you pay only as much as you owe and no more. **(Note to practitioners only: There is a fee of $10.00 for this publication.)**
   Forms 1040 (Schedules A, B, D, E, EIC, R), 1040A, 1040EZ, 2106, 2119, 2441, 3903, W-2.

Pub 334, Tax Guide for Small Business (For Individuals Who Use Schedule C or C-EZ)—explains federal tax laws that apply to sole proprietorships and statutory employees. **(Note to practitioners only: There is a fee of $6.50 for this publication.)**
   Forms 1040 (Schedules C, C-EZ, SE), 4562.

Other Publications

Pub 1, Your Rights as a Taxpayer—explains your rights at each step in the tax process. To ensure that you always receive fair treatment in tax matters, you should know what your rights are.

Pub 463, Travel, Entertainment, Gift, and Car Expenses—identifies business-related travel, entertainment, gift, and local transportation expenses that may be deductible.
   Forms 2106, 2106EZ.

Pub 501, Exemptions, Standard Deduction, and Filing Information—
   Forms 2120, 8332.

Pub 502, Medical and Dental Expenses—explains which medical and dental expenses are deductible, how to deduct them, and how to treat insurance reimbursements you may receive for medical care.
   Form 1040 (Schedule A).

Pub 503, Child and Dependent Care Expenses—explains that you may be able to take a credit if you pay someone to care for your dependent who is under age 13, your disabled dependent, or your disabled spouse. For purposes of the credit, "disabled" refers to persons physically or mentally unable to care for themselves. Tax rules covering benefits paid under a dependent care assistance plan are also explained.
   See Publication 926 for information on the employment taxes you may have to pay if you are a household employer.
   Forms 1040A (Schedule 2), 2441.

Pub 504, Divorced or Separated Individuals—Form 8332.

Pub 505, Tax Withholding and Estimated Tax—Forms 1040-ES, 2210, 2210F, W-4, W-4P, W-4S, W-4V.

Pub 508, Educational Expenses—identifies work-related educational expenses that may be deductible. Also discusses the exclusion for employer-provided educational assistance.
Forms 1040 (Schedule A), 2106, 2106EZ.

Pub 509, Tax Calendars for 1998

Pub 510, Excise Taxes for 1998—covers in detail the various federal excise taxes reported on Form 720. These include environmental taxes; facilities and service taxes on communications and air transportation; fuel taxes; manufacturers' taxes; vaccines; tax on heavy trucks, trailers, and tractors; luxury taxes; and tax on ship passengers. This publication briefly describes other excise taxes and which forms to use in reporting and paying the taxes.
Forms 11-C, 637, 720, 730, 6197, 6627.

Pub 520, Scholarship and Fellowships—explains the tax rules that apply to U.S. citizens and resident aliens who study, teach, or conduct research in the United States or abroad under scholarship and fellowship grants.
Forms 1040A, 1040EZ.

Pub 521, Moving Expenses—explains whether certain expenses of moving are deductible. For example, if you changed job locations last year or started a new job, you may be able to deduct your moving expenses. You also may be able to deduct expenses of moving to the United States if you retire while living and working overseas or if you are a survivor or dependent of a person who died while living and working overseas.
Forms 3903, 3903F, 4782.

Pub 523, Selling Your Home—explains how to treat any gain or loss from the sale of your main home.
Forms 2119, 8828.

Pub 525, Taxable and Nontaxable Income

Pub 526, Charitable Contributions—describes organizations that are qualified to receive charitable contributions. It also describes contributions you can (and cannot) deduct and explains deduction limits.
Forms 1040 (Schedule A), 8283.

Pub 527, Residential Rental Property—explains rental income and expenses and how to report them on your return. This publication also defines other special rules that apply to rental activity.
Forms 1040 (Schedule E), 4562.

Pub 529, Miscellaneous Deductions—identifies expenses you may be able to take as miscellaneous deductions on Form 1040 (Schedule A), such as employee business expenses and expenses of producing income. This publication does not discuss other itemized deductions, such as those for charitable contributions, moving expenses, interest, taxes, or medical and dental expenses.

Forms 1040 (Schedule A), 2106, 2106EZ.

Pub 530, Tax Information for First-Time Home Owners—

Forms 1040 (Schedule A), 8396.

Pub 533, Self-Employment Tax—explains how people who work for themselves figure and pay self-employment tax on their earned income. Self-employment tax consists of social security and Medicare taxes.

Form 1040 (Schedule SE).

Pub 550, Investment Income and Expenses—covers investment income such as interest and dividends, expenses related to investments, and sales and trades of investment property including capital gains and losses.

Forms 1040 (Schedules B, D), 1099-DIV, 1099-INT, 4952, 6781, 8815.

Pub 551, Basis of Assets—explains how to determine the basis of property, which is usually its cost.

Pub 552, Recordkeeping for Individuals—highlights and serves as a ready reference on general record keeping for individual income tax filing.

Pub 553, Highlights of 1997 Tax Changes

Pub 555, Community Property—provides helpful information to married taxpayers who reside in a community property state—Arizona, California, Idaho, Louisiana, Nevada, New Mexico, Texas, Washington, or Wisconsin. If you and your spouse file separate tax returns you should understand how community property laws affect the way you figure your income on your federal income tax return.

Pub 556, Examination of Returns, Appeal Rights, and Claims for Refund—

Forms 1040X, 1120X.

Pub 583, Starting a Business and Keeping Records—provides basic federal tax information for people who are starting a business. It also provides information on keeping records and illustrates a record keeping system.

Pub 587, Business Use of Your Home (Including Use by Day-Care Providers)—explains rules for claiming deductions for business use of your home and what expenses may be deducted.

Pub 590, Individual Retirement Arrangements (IRAs) (Including SEP IRAs and SIMPLE IRAs)—explains the tax rules that apply to IRAs and the penalties for not following them. Rules discussed include those affecting contributions, deductions, transfers (including rollovers), and withdrawals.

This publication also includes tax rules for Simplified Employee Pension (SEP) plans and Savings Incentive Match Plans for Employees (SIMPLE) plans.

Forms 1040, 1040A, 5329, 8606.

Pub 593, Tax Highlights for U.S. Citizens and Residents Going Abroad—provides a brief overview of various U.S. tax provisions that apply to U.S. citizens and resident aliens who live or work abroad and expect to receive income from foreign sources.

Pub 721, Tax Guide to U.S. Civil Service Retirement Benefits—

Forms 1040, 1040A.

Pub 926, Household Employer's Tax Guide (For Wages Paid in 1998)—identifies "household employees." Included are tax rules you should know about when you employ a household worker such as a baby-sitter, maid, yard worker, or similar domestic worker. This publication explains what taxes to withhold and pay and what records to keep.

Forms 1040 (Schedule H), W-2, W-3, W-4, W-5.

Pub 929, Tax Rules for Children and Dependents—explains filing requirements and the standard deduction amount for dependents. This publication also explains when and how a child's parents may include their child's interest and dividend income on their return and when and how a child's interest, dividends, and other investment income is taxed at the parents' tax rate.

Forms 8615, 8814.

Pub 936, Home Mortgage Interest Deduction—

Form 1040 (Schedule A).

Pub 950, Introduction to Estate and Gift Taxes—provides general information on the federal gift and estate tax. It explains when these taxes apply and how they can be eliminated by the unified credit.

Forms 706, 709.

Pub 957, Reporting Back Pay and Special Wage Payments to the Social Security Administration

Pub 967, The IRS Will Figure Your Tax—explains the procedures for choosing to have the IRS figure the tax on Forms 1040, 1040A, and 1040EZ.

Estate Planning

And now a few words about estate planning:

Paying attention to your money needn't end when you do. Do you want relatives fighting over your money? Wouldn't you like to help charities you admire, and receive tax benefits from doing so? Don't you want your estate to be as well organized as you are?

If you don't take care of your estate planning with a proper will, you'll have no control over your assets after your death, and everything will go through Intestate Secession Laws, which vary from state to state. In some states, all community property goes to your spouse, not your children—or, if you own property separately, the state may divide it, giving half to the child, half to the spouse; or, if you have two kids, two-thirds could go to the children, and one-third to the spouse. None of this may be what you had in mind.

So think about your life *and* your death. You can't take it with you, but you can make sure that others don't take it, either.

Some issues to consider:

It's important to plan your estate carefully. You'll learn more about your own priorities. Who is important to you? What are your values? Do you want to give money to your relatives, or to charities? Because estate planning forces you to look at your life, it can be an excellent vehicle for reflection.

Even if you're young, you need a plan. For instance, if you're 23 and unmarried, and you die, your assets may go to your parents, which might not make any sense. Leaving money to a sibling is considered more practical because, in estate planning, the flow of money generally tends to be downward, i.e., passing to younger generations. If you die at 23 and leave considerable assets to your parents, your property will be taxed first in your estate and then in theirs when they die (assuming they pass the money along to their surviving children).

And if you're young and have children, an estate plan is absolutely essential, because you must designate a guardian (although the court can turn down the request if it feels your choice isn't in the children's best interest). Otherwise, in the event of your death, the courts rely upon the law of the state in which you lived to determine who should act as guardian, which may be exactly what you *don't* want. Do you want your kids sent off to live with someone whom you loathe?

You should pay attention to estate planning as soon as you have assets. And don't let it lapse. This doesn't mean that you should see an estate planner every year, but what about after you've had a new child? Or your father has died? Or you've won the lottery?

Once your plan is in place, you should revisit it every few years or so. Life's circumstances change regularly, and so do finances. Not to mention the laws.

Understanding all your assets is a good start to establishing your estate plan. Your basic assets are: real estate; stocks, bonds, mutual-fund shares, and cash; tangible personal property, such as furniture, cars, and jewelry; business or investment partnership interests; jointly owned property in any of the above categories; life insurance; and retirement plans.

The Single Most Important Fact To Know: As of 1998, an estate with assets with less than $650,000 is, with a few exceptions, not subject to federal death taxes. Keep in mind that, although you may be well under the $650,000 limit now, by the time you die your assets may have accumulated enough interest to have grown past that mark.

The threshold for taxability is going to rise each year until 2000, when it reaches one million dollars.

Mind you, some states don't have a similar cutoff, but impose their own tax at other levels. Check and see if your state is one of them.

There is a marital deduction. If you're married, you can leave your spouse as much as you wish without paying taxes on it. A surviving spouse doesn't have to pay estate taxes until death, at which point the money will come out of his or her estate. (The exception is if your surviving spouse isn't a U.S. citizen. In that case, you'd need to give your property to a trust held in the United States.)

It's helpful to give money away. It's a great way to save on estate taxes. The American system of death and gift taxes is a unified one—in other words, the two have identical taxes and rates. A lifetime gift of $10,000 has the same structure as one bequeathed in a will.

From a tax viewpoint, there are four kinds of gifts:

1. **Untaxable cash gifts.** Throughout your life, you're allowed to give up to $10,000 annually to an unlimited number of recipients. If you're married and your spouse consents to the gift, together you can give up to $20,000.
2. **Ed/med gifts.** These are gifts paid directly to an educational or medical institution rather than to an individual.
3. **Gifts that use up the $650,000 tax exemption.** Example: Let's say you give your daughter $50,000. The first $10,000 of that is excluded from tax consideration. Now, you don't have to pay taxes on that other $40,000 today. But you *have* lost $40,000 of your $650,000 exemption. In other words, the IRS watches you throughout your lifetime. Just because 20 years have elapsed since you gave a gift, don't think that they won't remember. They're like elephants, without the charm. (By the way, the $650,000 exemption will go up every year until it hits $1,000,000.)
4. **Gifts that incur gift tax.** After you've used up all your tax exemptions, you'll owe tax on everything you give.

It's a good idea to establish a trust. There are many kinds of trusts, but basically they can be divided into two groups: **revocable** and **irrevocable**. Revocable trusts can be used as substitutes for wills and are used primarily to minimize delays due to probate. This type of trust offers no tax benefits.

Irrevocable trusts are exactly that: irreversible. They're designed to dictate the conditions of your estate and to avoid taxes (legally). You want to be pretty sure of yourself when you create one. You can't uncreate it.

There are many kinds of irrevocable trusts, and your estate planner can tell you which, if any, are best for you. They're usually only for those with estates over the $650,000 limit.

A revocable trust, or a **living trust**, is set up while you're alive. In it you place all your assets, including your money, your house, even your furniture. Your trustee then pays your bills and invests your money. As a result, your estate is no longer subject to probate administration, and so your estate's trustee can take immediate charge. For many people, avoiding probate can save money, as well as time.

Without a living trust, generally no one can access your property to pay your bills after your death until your will has been admitted to probate and an executor has been named. This kind of trust doesn't minimize estate taxes, however.

Ordinarily, if you become incapacitated and unable to manage your money, the court may have to appoint a guardian to take care of these duties. This is an expensive and intrusive process. A living trust enables you to avoid this, as you will have already named the person to act as your trustee if you are no longer able to handle your own affairs. You can also sign a durable power of attorney (see below).

Essentially, trusts allow you to control your property after your death: You decide, within limits, who receives what and when they receive it. If you want your spouse to think twice before remarrying after your death, you might provide that his rights to receive money from the trust cease upon his remarriage. But don't go crazy. Courts don't like wacky provisions. For instance, no matter how much you dislike your daughter-in-law, the courts would shy away from a provision requiring your son to slap her in public before he could receive benefits from the trust. Encouraging abuse is against public policy. It's bad enough to try to control others while you're alive, but don't try to do it from the grave.

Where there's a will, there's a way to make sense of your estate. So draw one up. It costs less than setting up a trust, but the amount varies. You can probably spend anywhere from $200 to $2,000 on a will. If it's done right, you save much more than that in the long run.

Keep your will in a safe place. If your lawyer maintains space in his or her office for wills, that's probably the best place. Many law firms rent vaults at banks or have separate safe storage areas for important documents. If your lawyer doesn't maintain such space, keep the will in a secure, fireproof place in your home. It isn't a good idea to store it in a safe-deposit box, because once you die, the laws in many states make it difficult for anyone to open the box until someone has been appointed executor of your estate (which cannot be done until the will is offered for probate). So if you insist on keeping you will in a box, consider giving someone else access.

You don't necessarily need a lawyer to draw up a will. If your estate is simple and your bequests minimal, some states allow you to create a holographic will. This means that it's handwritten. You should sign it, date it, and, if the state so requires, have it witnessed; then store it with your important papers.

Whatever state you live in, if your estate is small, you don't have minor children, and you want your property to pass as it would under the laws of intestacy, you may not need a will at all.

Insurance

Now that we've talked about what happens when you die, let's move on to another cheerful subject: How to lessen the effects of misfortune. Or, why you need insurance.

There are many kinds of insurance to consider. They are:

Life insurance. Replaces your wage income in the event of your death, covers estate taxes, and may be used for investment purposes.

Health insurance. Makes sure that your doctor bills don't make you feel sicker than your medical condition.

Automobile insurance. Covers your own liability if you injure someone else, covers your own medical and automobile repair costs if you are injured or your car is damaged, and can be used for financial protection against an incident involving someone who's uninsured.

Disability insurance. Replaces as much of your income as possible in case of a long-term disability.

Homeowner's insurance. Insures your property against theft or destruction. If you rent, renter's insurance similarly protects your personal property.

Personal liability insurance. Protects your personal assets from a personal liability law suit.

Professional liability insurance. Protects your professional assets from a job-related lawsuit.

Except for life insurance, which is not essential for everyone, all the others are necessary.

But first, as with any other kind of planning, think about the kind of agent you'd like to work with. You want her to possess the same qualities as any other professional: honesty, dependability, intelligence. And it doesn't hurt to find someone with a good deal of experience and the proper degrees. Ask for references. Does she know someone else who does what you do for a living?

How do you know whether your agent is good? The first sign is that she's been recommended by someone you know and trust. Your own instincts will tell you, too. Is she a good listener? She may not be brilliant, but if she's got good antennae, she'll know how to ask you the right questions to extract a sense of your particular needs, and she won't make any recommendations until she feels that she knows you well.

Now on to the different kinds of insurance. First comes health insurance, which may be the most important purchase you can make if you're single and aren't insured through your workplace. A bad illness can simply knock you out of the box. And then what? You end up a ward of the state. You no longer have a choice of doctor or treatment. Whenever I hear people say, "I can't afford medical insurance," I say, "No, you can't afford *not* to have it."

Many of the women I see tell me that they don't need to be concerned about health insurance because they're covered through their husband's employee-sponsored health plan. And often they're right. But it isn't enough to know coverage exists, as the extent of it varies widely. Examine the policy. Make sure the employer is giving you good benefits. If not, you can either lobby for change, or decide that you need an extra layer of protection, which is fairly inexpensive and can save you a bushel in the long run.

Something else to consider is long-term care insurance, which helps you look after yourself in the event that you have a prolonged illness or disability. Women often think that Medicare will cover all their nursing home expenses, but unfortunately, that's not so.

If you can afford it, your long-term policy should cover all kinds of nursing care rather than only under certain circumstances; it should last a lifetime rather than cover a limited period in a nursing home (after all, you probably won't want to leave the home when you reach 90); and it should cover all illnesses and conditions.

One tip: The younger you are when you buy such insurance, the cheaper it will be. A policy costing $500 a year when you're 45 could cost you many times that amount if purchased twenty-five years later.

Homeowner's insurance covers the property in your home, and protects your liability if someone is accidentally injured on your property. It also covers the money you spend while living in a hotel if your house burns down. If you rent, buy renter's insurance, for similar reasons.

Whether you get homeowner's or rental insurance, consider obtaining replacement-cost coverage, which means that the value of destroyed or lost items will be assessed based on what it would cost you to buy new ones, rather than on the current worth of the items themselves. Replacement insurance costs more, but it's worth it.

In order to ensure proper reimbursement, make a list of your possessions and a videotape of your valuable items. Note what your valuables are worth, and be as specific as possible. And if you buy expensive new items, keep the receipts and/or videotape them as well.

Auto insurance is fairly straightforward. Every state in the union requires you purchase some. So if you have a car, and you obey the law, you already have insurance.

But how do you know if your insurance is any good? You may well form a strong bond with the agent who works with you on your estate planning, life insurance, or disability insurance, but your auto-insurance agent usually won't give you more than a short conference.

What can you do? If you think life insurance is complicated, trying reading an automobile policy.

Don't be afraid to tackle the subject seriously. Interview a few agents. Ask them how long they've been in the business, what companies they like, and why they do business with them. If you ask an agent why she recommends a certain product, and she won't give you a straight answer, that's also bad. If she's a terrible listener, that's bad. Simply asking the questions is just as important as receiving the answers. It gives you a chance to see how that person handles you.

Your auto agent should be able to sort through all your options. Different states have different rules: Some require that you buy uninsured-motorist coverage, in case someone who's uninsured causes an accident. You should always have bodily injury, property liability, and medical payments insurance. But perhaps you don't need collision insurance, particularly if your car is old. And see whether your health coverage duplicates your medical payments auto coverage. Don't forget to look for discounts, too, which are available for those with good driving records or driver-training certificates, or who are senior citizens.

Some companies can sell you insurance directly, without having to use an agent. These companies can be very reputable, or not reputable at all, so be careful before you sign anything.

There are many different kinds of liability insurance, both personal and professional. One business owner may need protection in case someone slips in her lobby and breaks a leg, while another might need to guard against a wrongful-termination suit. Liability insurance is a very general term, and, in this litigious age, a necessity if you have any assets at all.

Personal liability insurance covers your nonwork life. Suppose someone comes to your house, trips over a nail in your foyer, breaks her leg and announces that she can no longer work. She then sues you for the income she would have made for the rest of her natural life. Liability insurance covers that suit. And it's not expensive.

Professional liability insurance is something all professionals should look into. If you're employed at a large firm, your company may provide it for you. Some professionals are more liable than others—doctors, lawyers, accountants, architects, and nurses among them.

Since personal liability insurance doesn't protect you from business-related liability, you need both types—and one way to make sure you have enough coverage is with an umbrella policy. This policy is exactly what it sounds like: a policy that extends your liability coverage in many areas. Umbrella policies are fairly cheap, perhaps $1,000 a year, and well worth it.

Then there's disability insurance, which is very important for anyone dependent on a working income. For a young person, the chances of becoming disabled are four times greater than the chances of dying. If you put ten people in a room, at least two of them will have a long-term disability over the next ten to twenty years. Almost half of all people now 35 years old will be incapacitated for three months or longer before they're 65.

The problem is that disability coverage has become such a hot item that there aren't enough insurance carriers to cover the demand. In other words, buying disability insurance is a little like sending your 16-year-old boy out to buy auto insurance. It's a sellers' market—unlike life insurance, which agents have to beg people to buy. Furthermore, it's gender-rated, which in this case means that it's more expensive for women than men. Sad but true, and there's nothing anyone can do about this.

How much should you have? It's very difficult to get disability insurance in high amounts—the companies usually want to cap your limit at 50 to 60 percent of your present earnings. So buy as much as you can get or afford. And beware: It's not cheap. Let's say you're earning $100,000 a year, and you want at least $5,000 a month, or 60 percent replacement. That might cost you as much as $3,000 to $3,500 a year in premiums.

Life insurance can be an essential part of any good financial portfolio, and it's also wildly complicated. The following explanation gives only the barest fundamentals.

All things considered, the type of life insurance product you choose should meet your needs and be affordable. Consider how much life insurance you truly require. If your spouse is your family's principal breadwinner, his insurance is more important than yours, and you and he should discuss whether you need it, too. You may not.

If you're single and no one's life will suffer from the loss of your income, your money would probably do better elsewhere.

If you're a single mother, or if you're the primary money-maker of the family, you probably do need life insurance. Perhaps the best way to determine this is to estimate how much money your family currently lives on, and determine what would happen to them financially if you were to die. You'd like your family to live well without you. As far as I'm concerned, that's life insurance's primary purpose.

You may have life insurance already through your employer—always check the benefits package when you take a job!

There are many other considerations with insurance, including various tax benefits and estate-planning benefits. There's no time to discuss those here, but make sure to ask your agent to tell you everything you ever need to know about insurance. In New York, Massachusetts, and Connecticut, you don't need an agent at all: Savings banks offer life insurance at low cost.

If using an agent is beyond your budget, you can buy your insurance through direct-marketing companies. You won't get as much advice, however, so this option is best for those who know their way around insurance, or who have been counseled by someone knowledgeable and simply want to buy a particular product.

Investments

Okay. You've taken care of your insurance, estate planning, and retirement needs. And you have enough money on hand for emergencies—most people say about three to six months' worth of monthly expenses will do. This money should be liquid, placed in a bank account or a money-market fund or a three-month T-bill (as we like to call a U.S. Treasury bill).

Now, after all this, if there's anything left, you can think about investing.

But what kind of investor do you think you'll be? For instance, are you the sort who won't go on a roller coaster? Do you prefer taking the car to making a quick trip on a small airplane? Or are you the sort who was bungee jumping before anyone else had even heard of it?

In other words, are you afraid of risk, or do you welcome it?

If you have the money, I want you to invest, no matter who you are. But some people are naturally inclined towards riskier portfolios than others. These people are usually the type who can sleep at night even if their investments are down 25 percent for the day, feeling confident that tomorrow will be better.

But there are other factors to consider besides your risk tolerance. These include how much time you're willing to give your investments, how much income you need, and so on.

One quick way to calculate who you are, investment-wise, is to take this short test.

1. What time horizon do you have for this investment? In other words, when do you want to be able to use the money for something other than as an investment?
   1. Short term (1 to 3 years)
   2. Medium term (4 to 7 years)
   3. Long term (more than 7 years)

2. If you require an income from this money, what annual percentage of it will you want?
   1. More than 4 percent
   2. 2 to 4 percent
   3. 1 to 2 percent
   4. None of it

3. During a down cycle in the market (such as the 23 percent decline of the S&P 500 in the crash of 1987), how much of a decline in the value of your portfolio do you think you could tolerate without having to seek professional help?

1. Less than 5 percent
2. 5 to 10 percent
3. 10 to 15 percent
4. 15 to 20 percent
5. More than 20 percent

4. If you had to pick between a strategy designed to produce high possible returns over the long run, but with lots of fluctuations, and a strategy that produces lower but more consistent and safe returns, which would you choose?
   1. Lower but more consistent returns
   2. Higher returns with more price fluctuations

5. Below are five portfolios with different potential risks and returns. Choose the portfolio that best reflects your risk tolerance for a quarterly decline in its value.

Portfolio	1. Conservative -Income	2. Moderate -Income	3. Moderate -Growth	4. Aggressive -Growth	5. Very Aggressive -Growth
Risk Tolerance*	0-5%	5-10%	10-15%	15-20%	20%·*
Down Market Risk**	3.9	6.1	11.8	18.0	21.8**
Historic Return	11.1	12.3	13.5	14.6	14.9

  * decline in portfolio in any quarter
  ** the largest decline in value from any single starting point through 12/95 based on quarterly return data

Okay. Now total the numeric value, based on the item number, of the answers you picked. If your answer totals:

Less than 6: Let's think about a conservative portfolio for you.
    6–10: You're in line for a moderate-income portfolio.
  11–15: You ought to consider a moderate-growth portfolio.
  15–17: You're a risk taker, which means you are attracted to an aggressive portfolio.
More than 17: You're very aggressive (so am I, by the way), and your portfolio should match.

Here are four different portfolios, from conservative to very aggressive. As you can see, the conservative portfolio contains more bonds than stock, while the aggressive portfolio contains only 20 percent bonds.

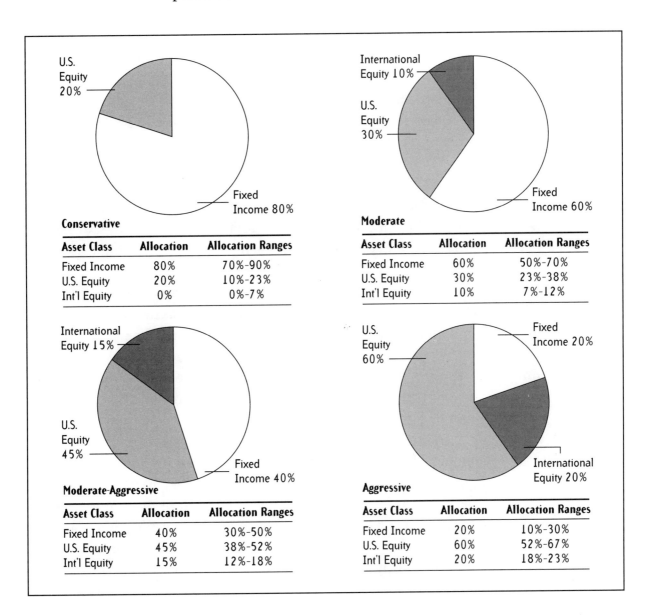

Conservative

Asset Class	Allocation	Allocation Ranges
Fixed Income	80%	70%-90%
U.S. Equity	20%	10%-23%
Int'l Equity	0%	0%-7%

Moderate

Asset Class	Allocation	Allocation Ranges
Fixed Income	60%	50%-70%
U.S. Equity	30%	23%-38%
Int'l Equity	10%	7%-12%

Moderate-Aggressive

Asset Class	Allocation	Allocation Ranges
Fixed Income	40%	30%-50%
U.S. Equity	45%	38%-52%
Int'l Equity	15%	12%-18%

Aggressive

Asset Class	Allocation	Allocation Ranges
Fixed Income	20%	10%-30%
U.S. Equity	60%	52%-67%
Int'l Equity	20%	18%-23%

Now that we know more about the kinds of investments you're willing to try, let's talk about the type of investments you can make.

There are four principal types of assets: stocks, bonds, cash (or cash equivalents), and real estate. (There are also assets which are more speculative, including commodity-type investments, such as oil or gas, and nonfinancial investments, including precious and nonprecious metals and collectibles, such as fine art and coins; these require an expert's hand.)

Real estate is not always the best investment for a beginner because it's not liquid. The most obvious way to invest in real estate is to buy a house in which to live; that way you can take advantage of the tax deductions for your mortgage payments, and you get to have a house, too. With any luck, your home will increase in value. Time is on your side if you live in your home, because the odds are good that you'll stay there for years—which allows more time for the house to appreciate in value.

Basically, cash is necessary for liquidity, bonds for income, and stocks for growth.

Cash and cash equivalents are liquid, low in risk, and low in return. They include checking accounts, certificate of deposit (CDs), and money market accounts.

As I mentioned, it's always good to have three to six months' worth of living expenses liquid. But there's no firm and fast rule that applies to everyone. Having that kind of money around is helpful, but one medical bill can eat up much of it in a gulp.

But if you do have enough money set aside for emergencies, and more to spare, you can now become an investor.

Bank CDs and checking accounts are insured by the Federal Deposit Insurance Corporation (FDIC) up to $100,000 per account. If your bank collapses, the FDIC will make sure you don't lose your money up to that limit.

A **bond** is basically a certificate that says you've lent somebody money. It's the formal equivalent of a handwritten IOU.

One good way to understand a bond is to compare it to a mortgage. If you own your own home, your debt is your mortgage. It's the equivalent to a bond that you issued. You borrowed a certain amount from the bank, and in return you've promised to pay it back in full plus interest at a certain percentage rate, in monthly installments over the course of, say fifteen to thirty years. If you don't follow through, the bank can take your house. That's called **secured debt.** Likewise, there are secured bonds, which are secured by assets such as real estate.

How do you know how much risk you're taking when you invest in a bond? The best way is to look at such well-regarded agencies as Standard & Poor's, or Moody's, which rate bond-issuing companies.

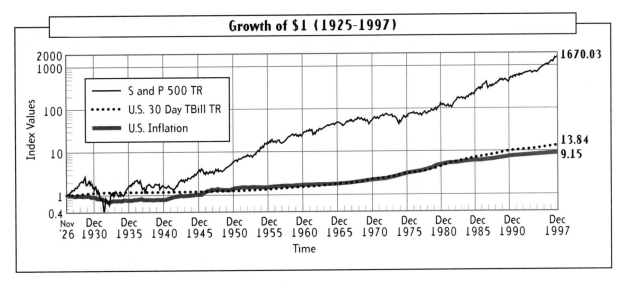

Growth of $1 (1925-1997)

Here we can see what has happened to one dollar over the course of the last fifty-two years in various vehicles:

    Standard & Poor's Long Term Index
    U.S. 30-Day Treasury Bill
    U.S. Small-Stock Total Return
    U.S. Long-Term Corporate Bond Total Return

And the rate of inflation over those same years.

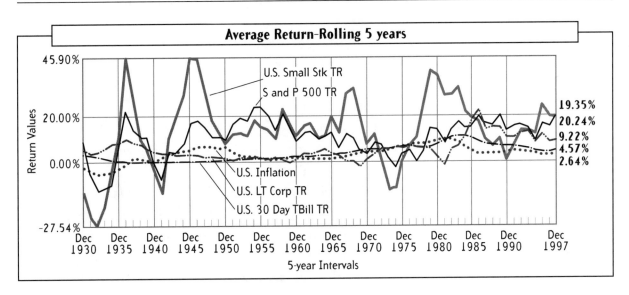

Average Return-Rolling 5 years

Here we can see the average return of these same vehicles, along with inflation, plotted for an average of five years. You can understand why I say you have to be able to deal with volatility. Although small stocks end up doing the best, they also have heartbreaking highs and lows during those five years, meaning that your investments may actually lose money before you make any. So remember "volatile" can also mean "profitable, long-term."

If you invest in both stocks and bonds, you come up with a portfolio that, not surprisingly, performs midway between a portfolio that is all stock (but volatile) and all bond (more conservative).

Credit Risk	Moody's	Standard & Poor's
Prime	Aaa	AAA
Excellent	Aa	AA
Upper medium	A-1, A	A
Lower medium	Baa-1, B	BBB
Speculative	BA	BB
Very speculative	B, Caa	B, CCC, CC
Default	Ca, C	D

Your creditor's creditworthiness determines how much you should get for loaning them money.

Bonds are also called fixed-income instruments, because they pay you a fixed amount of money on a regular basis, usually every six months, for the bond's life—unless the company goes out of business.

Bonds are also marketable. If you've bought a ten-year bond, you don't have to hold on to it for the entire ten years. But in order for bonds to change hands, they must have a price, just like anything else that you buy and sell. If that price is exactly the same as the face value—that is, if you buy a $10,000 bond for $10,000—that means you are buying it at what is called par. You're paying no more and no less than what you will get at maturity.

If, when you sell it, the price of your bond will be more than 100 percent of its face value, you'll be selling it at a premium. (Here is a second source of making money with your bond. The first is the interest you'll make from it. The second is selling the bond for what's known as a capital gain.)

However, the reverse also holds. Take the same scenario, except that this time the other bonds maturing when yours does are paying 8 percent. So, if you have to sell your 7-percent bond, naturally people will give you less than $10,000 for it. The other person is buying your bond at what is known as a discount.

Bonds can be issued by anyone who is deemed creditworthy — the government and its agencies, states, municipalities, foreign countries, and companies all over the world. Most of this investment universe is rated by the agencies mentioned above.

There's a "line" in the bond ratings that separates those investments that are considered higher quality from lower-quality investments. That line is called a Triple B by Standard & Poor's, or BBB.

Bonds rated above that line are said to be investment-grade. Bonds rated below that line are called high-yield bonds. The difference is that an investment-grade bond is of better quality, but pays less interest than that of a lower grade.

In other words, if GM issues bonds—or debt—this year, it might pay 8 percent interest. But if the WXY Widget Company issues bonds, and it's a new company with a short track record of earnings, they might have to pay an interest rate of 12 percent. If you're not a sophisticated investor, and you want to buy these higher-risk, lower-rated bonds for their higher yields, please do so through a professional or a mutual fund. This is one arena where it's easy to get burned. You really need good research.

Another common asset class is **stocks.**

The relationship between you, the stockholder, and the company that issues the stock is profoundly different from the relationship you have with your bond issuer. When you buy a bond, someone owes you money. This isn't true with stocks. When you buy a stock, you aren't guaranteed any income at all; you're not even guaranteed to get your money back.

A stock is the certificate of ownership of a certain proportion of the company. This type of ownership is also called equity.

In order to attract capital, some companies pay dividends to their stockholders, which means that they share a portion of their profits with you as they grow. A dividend is like an interest payment that the company pays you from its earnings. The amount and frequency of the dividends paid are at the discretion of the company, however, and you're not guaranteed any money at any time. In fact, there's no way to tell whether the company will pay any dividends at all.

Another kind of stock is called preferred stock, which is something of a mix between stocks and bonds. It pays dividends, so it creates income like bonds, but since it's also a stock, it has the capacity to appreciate. On the down side, the dividend isn't increased if the company makes profits, and the price of preferred stock moves more slowly than that of common stock.

Once you've bought your stock, the next step is to allow the market to evaluate it. Like bonds, most stocks are marketable; they can be sold easily. But since stocks go up and down, the stock's resale value depends on its price at the moment you wish to sell it. If this happens to be on a day when the market is booming, there's a good chance you'll sell it for a good price. If it's a depressed day for the market, you'll probably see less for it.

Even though your stock may go up in price, you won't realize your gains—or losses—until you actually sell.

You could buy a stock for $1,000, for instance, and watch it drop in value to $500, then see it rise again to $2,000. But since you haven't done anything with the stock during this time, this increase is called a paper gain, or a paper loss, and it's something that you don't need to follow closely. Traders monitor these movements, looking for as little as one-sixteenth of a point or less—but we're not traders. We're looking to build our net worth over time and grow our capital by having a prudent, smart invest-ment plan with long-term goals and a view to the future.

That's why it's important to have a philosophical view of stocks: Invest in the right companies, then sit back and allow them to evolve. Let the market do its thing.

How to Read a Stock Table

For all of you who've wondered what people are doing staring at those print-ridden pages in the financial sections: They're reading the stock charts. Now that you're going to be a stock owner, you should know how to read them too. Here's the code:

HIGH	LOW	STOCK	DIV	YLD	PE	VOL	HIGH	LOW	LST	CHG
$81^{11}/_{16}$	$48^5/_8$	GenElec	1.20	1.5	33	33302	$81^7/_{16}$	$80^1/_4$	$80^7/_{16}$	$-^{13}/_{16}$

- ▶ HIGH: the stock's highest price over the last 52 weeks
- ▶ LOW: the stock's lowest price over the last 52 weeks
- ▶ STOCK: the name of the stock (but not its symbol, in this case, GE)
- ▶ DIV: the annual dividend per share paid by the company
- ▶ YLD: Per cent yield tells you what kind of dividend you get as a percentage of the stock's current price. Here the yield is 1.5%.
- ▶ PE: the price-to-earnings ratio, which comes from dividing the stock's price per share by its earnings per share
- ▶ VOL: the number of shares sold during the day, in thousands
- ▶ HIGH, LOW, LST: the weekly high, weekly low, and the final price the day before
- ▶ CHG: the difference between the last day's closing price and the closing price for the day before that

As I've mentioned, many women are afraid to go near the stock market. They agree with my father, who thought investing in stocks was a form of gambling, and preferred to bet on dice. But the difference between the two is that when you play craps, you're depending solely on luck; when you choose a stock, you rely on good research, sound knowledge, and proven strategies.

The best approach for making money consistently is called diversification. This is a concept we've been hearing about all our lives, only using different words and referring to many different situations. Those words are: Don't put all your eggs in one basket.

You reach diversification in investing through careful asset allocation, which means distributing your investment dollar among different investment (asset) classes.

The principal asset classes we discussed earlier can be broken down into more specific classes, such as by economic sector, by region, by quality, and so on.

To make sure that you aren't tied to one particular area, you should spread your investments around. You should buy conservative securities as well as others that give you growth. You may want some investments in one part of the world, and some in another. You should have stocks in different industries, too, even though they may appear to have more risk attached. Just by making sure that your investments are spread over a range of options, you're taking an enormously important step toward guaranteeing your success.

A simple way to start asset allocation is through what's called the institutional asset allocation, a formula used by most pension funds and balanced mutual funds. This consists of a portfolio composed of 60 percent stocks and 40 percent bonds, in addition to whatever cash you have. It's a simple and rational method that gives you some income, through the bonds, and some growth, through the stocks.

It's a constant trade-off, growth and income, income and growth. When you want income, you often give up growth. When you want growth, you don't get as much income.

How Much Are CDs Really Worth?

If you've got money, but you don't think you have to go into the stock market because your CD is paying a high interest rate, think again. After inflation and taxes, you might be well be losing money. Here you can see how much a CD was really worth over the past twenty years. Even in 1980, when CDs were paying an astronomical 13.67 percent, after taxes and inflation, you were still losing 4.34 on your money.

Year	CD Rate	CD Rate After Inflation	CD After Tax	CD After Tax & Inflation
1978	8.10	-0.85	4.85	-4.09
1979	11.45	-1.64	6.87	-6.22
1980	13.67	1.13	8.20	-4.34
1981	17.63	7.98	10.58	0.93
1982	13.59	9.35	8.15	3.91
1983	9.52	5.52	5.71	1.71
1984	11.06	6.84	6.64	2.42
1985	8.59	4.64	5.15	1.20
1986	7.02	5.82	4.21	3.01
1987	6.92	2.40	4.15	-0.37
1988	7.92	3.36	4.75	0.19
1989	9.70	4.82	5.82	0.94
1990	8.63	2.38	6.18	-1.07
1991	6.57	3.40	3.94	0.77
1992	4.05	1.12	2.43	-0.50
1993	3.32	0.56	1.99	-0.77
1994	4.46	1.74	2.68	-0.04
1995	6.24	3.61	3.74	1.11
1996	5.63	2.23	3.38	-0.02
1997	5.78	4.01	3.47	1.70

The Rich Is Better Workbook

Tax-Free Vehicle Yields

You always hear about tax-free vehicles that allow you to accumulate interest on your investments without your having to pay taxes. How much do they really make for you? You can use this table to find out.

Let's say you've got a tax-free vehicle such as a municipal bond that pays 5 percent interest, and you're in the 28 percent tax bracket. That means that your 5 percent would be the equivalent of 6.94 percent if you had to pay taxes on it. And if you're in the 39.6 percent tax bracket, and your bond happens to pay 14 percent, that's the equivalent of a 23.18 percent investment. Nice work!

TAX BRACKET	15.00%	28.00%	31.00%	33.00%	36.00%	39.60%
4.00%	4.71%	5.56%	5.80%	5.97%	6.25%	6.62%
4.25%	5.00%	5.90%	6.16%	6.34%	6.64%	7.04%
4.50%	5.29%	6.25%	6.52%	6.72%	7.03%	7.45%
4.75%	5.59%	6.60%	6.88%	7.09%	7.42%	7.86%
5.00%	5.88%	6.94%	7.25%	7.46%	7.81%	8.28%
5.25%	6.18%	7.29%	7.61%	7.84%	8.20%	8.69%
5.50%	6.47%	7.64%	7.97%	8.21%	8.59%	9.11%
5.75%	6.76%	7.99%	8.33%	8.58%	8.98%	9.52%
6.00%	7.06%	8.33%	8.70%	8.96%	9.38%	9.93%
6.25%	7.35%	8.68%	9.06%	9.33%	9.77%	10.35%
6.50%	7.65%	9.03%	9.42%	9.70%	10.16%	10.76%
6.75%	7.94%	9.38%	9.78%	10.07%	10.55%	11.18%
7.00%	8.24%	9.72%	10.14%	10.45%	10.94%	11.59%
7.25%	8.53%	10.07%	10.51%	10.82%	11.33%	12.00%
7.50%	8.82%	10.42%	10.87%	11.19%	11.72%	12.42%
7.75%	9.12%	10.76%	11.23%	11.57%	12.11%	12.83%
8.00%	9.41%	11.11%	11.59%	11.94%	12.50%	13.25%
8.25%	9.71%	11.46%	11.96%	12.31%	12.89%	13.66%
8.50%	10.00%	11.81%	12.32%	12.69%	13.28%	14.07%
8.75%	10.29%	12.15%	12.68%	13.06%	13.67%	14.49%
9.00%	10.59%	12.50%	13.04%	13.43%	14.06%	14.90%
9.25%	10.88%	12.85%	13.41%	13.81%	14.45%	15.31%
9.50%	11.18%	13.19%	13.77%	14.18%	14.84%	15.73%
9.75%	11.47%	13.54%	14.13%	14.55%	15.23%	16.14%
10.00%	11.76%	13.89%	14.49%	14.93%	15.62%	16.56%
10.25%	12.06%	14.24%	14.86%	15.30%	16.02%	16.97%

(continued)

TAX BRACKET	15.00%	28.00%	31.00%	33.00%	36.00%	39.60%
10.50%	12.35%	14.58%	15.22%	15.67%	16.41%	17.38%
10.75%	12.65%	14.93%	15.58%	16.04%	16.80%	17.80%
11.00%	12.94%	15.28%	15.94%	16.42%	17.19%	18.21%
11.25%	13.24%	15.62%	16.30%	16.79%	17.58%	18.63%
11.50%	13.53%	15.97%	16.67%	17.16%	17.97%	19.04%
11.75%	13.82%	16.32%	17.03%	17.54%	18.36%	19.45%
12.00%	14.12%	16.67%	17.39%	17.91%	18.75%	19.87%
12.25%	14.41%	17.01%	17.75%	18.28%	19.14%	20.28%
12.50%	14.71%	17.36%	18.12%	18.66%	19.53%	20.70%
12.75%	15.00%	17.71%	18.48%	19.03%	19.92%	21.11%
13.00%	15.29%	18.06%	18.84%	19.40%	20.31%	21.52%
13.25%	15.59%	18.40%	19.20%	19.78%	20.70%	21.94%
13.50%	15.88%	18.75%	19.57%	20.15%	21.09%	22.35%
13.75%	16.18%	19.10%	19.93%	20.52%	21.48%	22.76%
14.00%	16.47%	19.44%	20.29%	20.90%	21.87%	23.18%

Knowing that you have to think about diversifying your investments, your next step is to decide what to buy. If you have $200,000 or more, it might be worthwhile hiring an asset manager.

The three fundamental alternatives are: individual bonds and individual stocks, which we've discussed, and mutual funds.

As of this moment there are more than 7,000 mutual funds. By the time you read this, there may be a few hundred more, while some of the existing ones will have closed. Basically, these funds are pools of assets (investors' money) managed by a particular manager or team that uses a clearly defined and publicly disclosed investment policy, and is registered through the Securities and Exchange Commission (SEC).

As an investor, when you buy a mutual fund, you're buying units, or shares, of this particular pool. These shares are like the shares of an investment company; you're now a holder of a certain proportion of the investments in this pool.

There are two different types of funds: open-end funds and closed-end funds. Open-end funds take money every day. You can buy into the fund or liquidate your units daily, at the net asset value (see page 136). Closed-end funds have a fixed number of shares that are usually listed on a major stock exchange. They also have a limited period during which they will take investor's money directly.

One of the greatest advantages of owning shares in a mutual fund is that you're relieved from making detailed investment decisions; your only decision is into which asset classes you'll put your money—stocks, bonds, subclasses, or mixes of these.

You aren't involved in choosing the actual security (which means anything traded openly on the market). The fund manager does that for you, and since the pool holds a large amount of money, it can diversify and protect you more than you could do yourself with your own, say, $10,000. That $10,000 worth of stocks and bonds buys you a few positions, but in a mutual fund it can give you many positions, because you own a small piece of a big pool of investments.

Another advantage of a fund is that you don't have to be a genius to prosper. Fund managers are professionals who spend all their time reading and analyzing the market so that you don't have to. If I had elbow pain, I wouldn't buy a book to figure out how to make it feel better. I'd go to a doctor who understands joints. Even if you don't want to learn that much about finance yourself, or to hire an adviser, you can afford a mutual fund, which gives you that kind of assistance.

The range of mutual funds is extensive. Most funds stick to a certain specialty, such as large-cap stocks, growth stocks, municipal bonds, high-yield junk bonds, foreign stocks, or even gold and silver. Others create balanced mixes. Some mutual-fund companies sell directly to the consumer, while some charge sales fees and sell through brokers or other agents.

Thus you can pick a fund in any of the asset classes in which you've decided to invest. Or better yet, pick a few, and diversify yourself right from the start. In other words, allocate your money yourself, putting perhaps 45 percent into a bond fund, 20 percent into a large-capitalization stock fund, 15 percent into a small-cap stock fund, 10 percent into a foreign-stock fund, and the remaining 10 percent into two others that you've heard about and like.

Many mutual-fund companies sell their units directly to consumers without using intermediaries and without charging fees. There are always management expenses, however, and these are disclosed in the fund's annual report. The price of the unit, known as the net asset value, which is published every day, is calculated after taking into account these management fees and expenses.

When you buy directly from the fund, you are generally purchasing what is called a no-load fund. This means there are no extra fees other than the fund's management costs, which are reflected in the net asset value.

As mentioned, many fund companies don't distribute to the public, nor do they want to be salespeople, so they employ intermediaries. Since these intermediaries also have to make money, you incur additional expenses by using them.

Once these intermediaries were brokerage firms only, but now they also consist of banks, investment advisers, insurance companies, and so forth. In return for a fee—or, in a broker's case, a commission—they offer you recommendations on which funds to buy and sell, as well as manage the process for you. Loads, or fees, can range from 3/4 of a percent to 8 percent, and by law they must be disclosed to you by your broker or adviser.

These fees are usually front load, indicating that you pay right away; or back end, meaning that you pay when you sell the fund units.

For the most part, the no-load fund companies offer you no advice, although this custom is changing. But generally, no-load means no advice and no fee, and load means advice with a fee.

Now consider this: If you invest $100 in a 5 percent front-loaded fund, out of $100 you're actually investing only $95. So, after a nice yearly return of 10 percent, instead of making $10, you've made 10 percent of $95, or $9.50. Thus you may feel obliged to stay in this investment for several years in order to amortize your load—in other words, to spread the cost of the 5 percent sales charge over time, to make up for the money you spent in year one.

Similarly, you may not want to sell a back-end fund for a long time, because you don't want to pay the fee. This reluctance to sell may color the way you handle your investments, and it certainly can affect your return.

So the load can influence your money-making capability, as well as your psychology.

Beyond that, here's something else to remember: We're all human beings. That same intermediary who last year sold you a fund with a 5 percent front load may tell you this year to buy a different one. It's not his money, after all, and he gets a new commission. You must be alert when you're operating in the load arena. Otherwise, you may find yourself paying out more in fees than is worthwhile.

Some Major No-Load Mutual-Fund Companies

Boston Company Advisors Group
One Boston Place
Boston, MA 02108
(800) 225-5267

Columbia Funds Management Co.
1301 SW Fifth
P.O. Box 1350
Portland, OR 97207
(800) 547-1707

Dreyfus Corporation
1299 Ocean Avenue, Suite 650
Santa Monica, CA 90401
(213) 395-8005

Evergreen Asset Management Corporation
2500 Westchester Avenue
Purchase, NY 10577
(800) 235-2423

Fidelity Management and Research Corp.
82 Devonshire Street
Boston, MA 02109
(800) 522-7297

Founders Asset Management
2930 East Third Avenue
Denver, CO 80206
(800) 525-2440

Janus Capital
100 Fillmore Street
Denver, CO 80206
(800) 525-3713

Jones & Babson, Inc.
Three Crown Center
2440 Pershing Road
Kansas City, MO 64108
(800) 422-2766

Nicholas Company
700 Water Street
Milwaukee, WI 53202
(414) 272-6133

SAFECO Mutual Funds
P.O. Box 348990
Seattle, WA 98124
(800) 426-6730

The Scudder Funds
P.O. Box 2291
Boston, MA 02107
(800) 225-2470

Value Line
711 Third Avenue
New York, NY 10017
(800) 223-0818

Vanguard Group
Vanguard Financial Center
P.O. Box 2600
Valley Forge, PA 19482
(800) 662-7447

Brokers and Money Managers

For many of you, paying full attention to your investments is out of the question. You're too busy. There's nothing wrong with asking a broker to carry out your transactions for you: It's no different from having any other professional in your life.

There are a few factors to consider, however.

When you give a stockbroker discretion, you're letting her buy or sell a stock without telling you about each transaction (although you will always receive a confirmation at a later date). Therefore, before handing over such discretion, you must investigate this person's reputation and her track record. Get to know her. Ask questions. Disreputable people populate every industry, and this one is no exception, but if you do your homework and deal with a good firm with a good reputation, the odds are in your favor that your broker will be honest as well as helpful.

If you feel your broker isn't serving you well, talk to her office manager, as well as to the company's compliance officer, who ensures that the firm obeys the rules set by the Securities and Exchange Commission (SEC) and the National Association of Securities Dealers (NASD). You can also call the NASD hot line at (800) 289-9999.

If you do give your broker full discretion, check in with her every three to six months. And read your statements carefully. So many women say, "Don't make me read that piece of paper with all the numbers on it." If you feel you won't understand, then have your broker help you with it. It's not that complicated. And it *is* your money.

Read your stock-trade confirmations, too. Don't tell me you didn't know your broker bought you such-and-such a stock and that you hate that kind of stock and wish she hadn't bought it. The only reason you didn't know was that you didn't bother to open your mail and read the confirmation.

If you see something peculiar on your statement, ask questions. You get a physical every year, and if something odd turns up, you ask. Likewise, if something odd happens to your money, ask. You can address a problem right away if you're paying attention.

Another factor to consider in selecting the right broker is objectivity: You want someone who will choose investments impartially. Make sure that she isn't selling you only her own firm's prod-

Having Trouble with Your Securities?

Don't just fret! Call someone. Specifically:

U.S. Securities and Exchange
Commission
Office of Consumer Affairs
450 Fifth Street, NW
Washington, DC 20549
(202) 942-7040

Northeast Regional Office
7 World Trade Center
New York, NY 10048
(212) 748-8000

Boston District Office
73 Tremont Street
Boston, MA 02108
(617) 424-5900

Philadelphia District Office
601 Walnut Street
Philadelphia, PA 19106
(215) 597-3100

Southeast Regional Office
1401 Brickell Avenue
Miami, FL 33131
(305) 536-5765

Atlanta District Office
3475 Lenox Road NE
Atlanta, GA 30326
(404) 842-7600

Midwest Regional Office
500 West Madison Street
Chicago, IL 60661
(312) 353-7390

Central Regional Office
1801 California Street
Denver, CO 80202
(303) 391-6800

Fort Worth District Office
801 Cherry Street
Fort Worth, TX 76102
(817) 334-3821

Pacific Regional Office
5670 Wilshire Boulevard
Los Angeles, CA 90036
(213) 965-3998

San Francisco District Office
44 Montgomery Street
San Francisco, CA 94104
(415) 705-2500

And if you're having problems
specifically with your broker,
call the National Association of
Securities Dealers (NASD):

Executive Office
NASD, Inc.
1735 K Street NW
Washington, DC 20006-1506
(202) 728-8400

You can also call one of the
district offices:

District 1
1 Union Square
600 University Avenue
Seattle, WA 98101
(206) 624-0790

District 2N
425 California Street
San Francisco, CA 94104
(415) 781-3434

District 2S
300 South Grand Avenue
Los Angeles, CA 90071

District 3
1401 17th Street
Denver, CO 80202
(303) 298-7234

District 4
12 Wyandotte Plaza
120 W. 12th Street
Kansas City, MO 64105
(816) 421-5700

District 5
Energy Center
1100 Poydras Street
New Orleans, LA 70163

District 6
Olympia and York Tower
1999 Bryan Street
Dallas, TX 75201
(214) 969-7050

District 7
One Securities Center
3490 Piedmost Road
Atlanta, GA 30305

District 8
10 South La Salle
Chicago IL 60603
(312) 899-4400

District 9
1940 East 6th Street
Cleveland, OH 44114
(216) 694-4545

District 10
1735 K Street NW
Washington, DC 20006
(202) 665-1180

District 11
1818 Market Street
Philadelphia, PA 19103
(215) 665-1180

District 12
NASD Financial Center
33 Whitehall Street
New York, NY 10004
(212) 858-4000

District 13
260 Franklin Street
Boston, MA 02110
(617) 439-4404

ucts, nor should she be bound by a limited array of options within her own firm. And keep in mind the structure of her compensation. If she's earning commissions from your investments, that may color her advice. Also, she'll be receiving no commissions when she's doing nothing—i.e., neither buying nor selling anything for you. Yet there are many times when doing nothing is exactly the right course of action—sometimes for very long periods of time.

Let's say that you decide you need more than a stockbroker. Perhaps you would prefer to hire someone to manage your entire investment portfolio.

The major difference between a brokerage account and a money-management account is that whenever your broker performs a transaction, you pay a commission. An asset manager, however, charges you a fee based on a percentage of the money under her management. She makes her money by performing well for you: The more money you make, the more she makes. The benefit here is that you always know your costs, because the fee is a constant percentage. It can range from 3/4 of a percent to 3 percent, depending on the size of your account (the larger the account, the smaller the percentage fee).

Generally, you need $200,000 or more to hire an asset manager, although there are always exceptions.

When you first meet a manager—and you should interview several to find one you like—try to understand her approach, her policy, her philosophy. Find out about her track record over the years. Make sure that she understands your objectives, time horizon, and expectations. In other words, is she listening to you or just trying to sell you?

Once you've made a selection, let her do her thing. You must maintain good communication, but you don't have to talk every day. Once every few months may be enough.

Another benefit of having an asset manager is that you eliminate the possible conflict of interest a broker might have, because there are no transaction charges. That means the manager doesn't make money every time you buy or sell. Her incentive to do well derives from the percentage of your money that she receives as her fee. Your success is her success.

Asset management is not necessarily preferable to a brokerage account. It's simply another way to take care of your money.

There are many outlets to help you manage your money with input from various advisers, and under a variety of pricing arrangements. There are, for example, investment advisers who will design and supervise a portfolio of investments for you, charging a percentage of assets as an annual fee. They may work with other money managers or brokers, or manage the funds themselves. Some investment advisers, usually consultants, may charge an hourly fee; and you can use their services as the need arises.

No arrangement relieves you of responsibility regarding your portfolio. You still need to study your quarterly statements. Try to become familiar with indexes (such as the Standard & Poor's 500) that reflect average market movement. Few people make money when everyone else is losing money, but you don't want to lose money when everyone else is making it.

5

JUDY'S FAQS OF LIFE (FREQUENTLY ASKED QUESTIONS)

Whenever I go out on the road, I'm besieged with questions from women of all ages, stripes, and climes about everything from the best way to invest money to the best bond options to the right clothes to wear to work. I've even been asked whether or not I thought a certain marriage was healthy, implying that somehow I had the experience to decide such issues. I don't. No one has all the answers to every question. But I do have some answers to questions about money, so I thought I should share at least some of the ones I hear most often.

Keep in mind there are a few things I can't help you with. Sometimes it seems—particularly when you watch television talk shows—that certain people can predict the country's financial future. They can't. No one can. I'd love to be able to tell you that there's a big boom coming, or that the economy's heading for a downturn. But I can't do that, and I won't even try. Be careful of anyone who claims to know what the future holds. Plenty of people can make enlightened guesses, and many times they'll be right. But anyone who guarantees that she knows what's going to happen tomorrow is someone whom I guarantee you can't trust today.

Nor can I tell you what's precisely right for you and your money. So many times women have come up to me after a lecture and asked, "What should I do with my money?" There may not be a precise answer. But I can offer many guidelines and advice and tell you stories from my own experiences in hopes that they will be similar to yours. And I can tell you about the experiences of women I've met while giving my seminars and touring the country for my book.

Now, if you have more questions after reading this section, please contact me via my Web site at http://www.judyresnick.com.

I'm afraid of numbers. Won't that make it impossible for me to get involved in financial matters?

Not at all. I had exactly the same phobia. I hated mathematics. But when the time came that I *had* to work with numbers, I did, and I did it as well as anyone else. And that's what you'll discover, too. It's not that hard. That's why they teach math in elementary school. The only difference is that now you don't have to worry about showing off your ability in front of boys.

Anyway, these days there's such a thing as a calculator. So if you're really blocked, all you have to do is take out a little machine. Everything I was afraid of for years my 7-year-old granddaughter can do on a calculator—and she loves it. So can you.

But my mother always told me that women who are good with numbers are bad with people. In other words, men don't like those kinds of women.

Yes, and she might have also told you to wear a girdle so that your tushie wouldn't shake. Or not to leave your husband's bed, no matter what he does. Or never to speak in the company of strangers. And so on. Our mothers knew a lot, but there were some things they didn't know. It's time to move on. The next time your mother comes over, show her that you can balance her checkbook and translate her financial statements, and maybe she'll change her mind about math. Tell her it's never too late to enroll in a continuing-education class. Who knows? Maybe, if she's single, she'll meet a nice man.

And if you were told you couldn't expect to understand math

not by your mother but by a teacher, the same advice applies. A lot of us heard that. Even my own father once looked me in the eye and said he wished that I had been born a male, because then, and only then, could I take over his business. Ha! If you accept that mentality, you'll end up living in the nineteenth century.

I'm afraid to examine what I have—what if it turns out that I'm losing money every month because I'm spending too much, or because I haven't invested my money in a good place?

_____

That's exactly why you have to examine it. Remember, reality is your best friend. It's your job to find out what's going on with your financial health, just as it's your job to find out what's happening to your physical health. You don't avoid Pap smears because you're afraid of the results—or do you?

You're not being good to yourself if you're not taking care of your money just as you would any other part of your being, whether it be your head, your heart, your body, or your soul. So yes, maybe you'll get some bad news. That's just the first step toward making everything better.

I'd like to start, but my papers are strewn all over the house, I don't know where my files are, and I'm not sure if I have any tax records. Should I bother?

_____

Of course. I hear this type of comment all the time from women, and they remind me of overweight women who say it's too late to diet. It's never too late! You have to start somewhere. And while I'm not sure that diets really work (they never seem to for me, and I've been trying them all my life), organization does. So get organized. That's the key. Begin now. If your records aren't in one place, get them there. If you must, hire someone to help—either as a one-time chore or every year.

Or learn to use a computer, if you haven't already. There are all kinds of great programs that can handle your checks, your accounting—anything you need to do. If you think you can't do something, your computer can.

I want to become more involved in my money matters, but my husband is against it. He says that he's taking care of everything and that I don't need to worry. So I don't. Should I?

If he's got the information all organized and prepared, then you don't have to intrude on his system. But you can ask to be included. Tell him you're pleased that he's worked so hard, but you'd just like to look it over and become more familiar with it.

If asking for something this basic causes trouble, then I don't know what to tell you. I don't give marital advice, but my sense is that if you can't at least ask to see what's happening with your own finances, maybe you have issues calling for marriage counseling rather than tax counseling. It's not as if you're saying, "I want to take this over from you, you jerk." You're saying, "Sweetheart, I'd really feel much safer if I understood where we stood financially." There's a difference.

My husband manages the finances but I know he's spending too much.

Overspending is not gender-related. Anyone can waste money, regardless of sex, age, or income level. I've run into plenty of women whose family finances would be a great deal healthier if the man of the house weren't out there running up the accounts for toys such as snowmobiles and fancy CD players.

So ask him not to. Suggest that both of you work within a budget. If you can't talk to your husband that openly about your finances, then maybe there's an interpersonal issue at hand. He's throwing your money away. Ask him why. Is there some pathology at work? A lot of people have weird problems related to money. I know one woman who, whenever she becomes sick, goes out and spends everything she has. It makes her feel better. A male friend of mine can't resist buying new cars. He doesn't need more than one, but he's got four, and I'm sure he'll buy another soon. If I were Freud, I might be able to come up with an easy answer to this question, but I'm not, so I can't. All I can say is: Don't let these issues get the best of you. Too many people who could be financially secure are not, because they can't stop spending. So whether it's you or your spouse who's doing it, if you can't stop, then consider professional help. In the long run, that's going to cost a lot less than ten new cars.

I'm about to get married, and my husband wants to merge our accounts. Is this a good idea?

Why do so many women ask me this? I guess when you get married, there are so many things to think about, and so many questions to ask, that you're always looking for absolute answers where there are none—like this one. There is no right or wrong here. I can only talk from personal experience. I prefer to have my own bank account and let him have his, along with a joint account. After a while the joint account should grow the most. Simply put, it's never a bad idea to keep some property separate.

One of the first things to do when you're setting up your household is to sit down and make a plan together. When I got married in 1961, men and women didn't do that. If they had, I think many more marriages would have survived. But today's another story, so go ahead. Just as you sit down and talk about how you feel about children, or a home, or your in-laws. How do you feel about money? Address the issue right away, so that you get it out in the open.

How a person handles money speaks volumes. Are you an overspender, a miser, a balanced saver? Get it out there and talk about it. Talk first, spend later.

I hear what you're saying about saving money and investing wisely, but I can't do that, because even though I'm 40 and I make a lot of money, I spend every penny the moment I get it.

This is a question I field now and then, and unfortunately my usual response is this: Take some of that money and see a therapist. If you're really spending everything you make at the age of 40, you're living in a dream world. You need a dose of reality.

You keep talking about saving, but so much else comes up in life. I want to travel, I want to buy a nice new suit. I need to have so many things.

Not true. You don't have to have anything. You *want* to have things. Go to a poor neighborhood and ask the women there what they "have" to have. Sometimes you just have to make choices between what you want and what you need. I've had to teach this to myself. If I want this, maybe I have to give up that. Life is filled with trade-offs. If I want to be thin, I can't eat ice cream; if I want to have children, I can't take a job that puts me on the road fifty weeks a year, and so on.

So, maybe you *want* that vacation, but you *need* that savings account. Your needs are more important than your wants.

But if I don't buy those beautiful dresses and go to an expensive salon, no man will be attracted to me.

Face facts. Armani suits don't help you catch a man. A hairdo doesn't catch a man. *You* do: your personality, your soul, your being. Anyway, if you *do* catch a man by doing phony things, what happens one day when you don't look like the million dollars you just spent on yourself? You won't be able to keep him anyway.

How can I ever save money when they keep sending me all those credit cards?

If someone hands you poison, are you going to eat it? No. If you can't handle a credit card, then it's poison to you. Rip it up. You have to learn to say no in this world, and you have to say no to yourself.

My own personal hell is eating healthy. I love food. I could eat all day and all night. I just moved to a new house, and only a few blocks away there's a candy store with the world's best chocolate. It's killing me. I want something every time I walk by. But I know if I give in, I'll gain weight. It's a choice. Happy for a moment, miserable for a month. You decide.

I came of age in the 1960s and I still believe a lot of sixties' teachings. One of those ideas is that money is the root of all evil.

Not quite. The actual quotation is: "The love of money is the root of all evil" (1 Tim. 6:10). In other words, it's not having money, or making money, but adoring money that gets you into trouble.

Anyway, I don't want you to love money. I want you to love yourself. And I want you to believe that because you love yourself so much, you can take care of yourself. Too many of us were raised to believe that someone else was supposed to provide for us, someone else was supposed to love us. It doesn't always work that way. As far as I'm concerned, I love myself when I provide for myself.

People who love money are usually greedy and would do anything to get it. But not all people who *have* money are greedy. Many are very generous and charitable. Money used properly is a wonderful thing. You can adhere to any benevolent value system you like, and still have time to watch over and grow your money.

At one time I was a real 1960s hippie. When my father told me he'd voted for Nixon, I couldn't even look at him. I couldn't believe he would do such a thing. A Republican! Finally my dad said, "You think my money's dirty, but you know something? It's feeding you, it's clothing you, it's taking care of you."

He was right. Just because he had money (and voted strangely) didn't mean he wasn't a wonderful person. So go ahead. Be a great old sixties person, become rich, and then do something special with your money. But make sure that part of what you do is take care of yourself. Because that's being truly special. Even hippies used to say, "Grow your own garden first."

I have a terrible self-image. My mom always said I couldn't do anything. I don't envision myself as financially successful. I'm always someone else's assistant. That's as far as I'll ever go.

I can't argue with your feelings, but I also don't think you're alone with them. Many women have grown up with a negative sense of self. I was certainly one of them. I didn't think I could ever do anything, either. I discovered whatever abilities I have only by accident, after I lost all my money and went out interviewing for a job. Because I was so afraid of being destitute, I decided I couldn't afford to be an assistant, because I wouldn't earn enough money from it.

So I went out with a positive attitude. And when the men at my first interviews looked at me as though I wanted to be a secretary, I made it clear that wasn't the case. Someone once told me that if you act like an assistant that's what you'll be. Sometimes you have to fake it—just as you sometimes have to fake other things.

Women can remain feminine (if they wish to), become mothers (if they wish to), and take care of their money at the same time. It's not overwhelming. Your mother was wrong. Own up to it.

My father told me I was too dumb to have anything to do with my own money. Now he's in a nursing home, and I don't have any choice but to take care of our finances—but I'm still scared.

But look at what being scared really means. For instance, would you rather take a thousand dollars and put it under your mattress and not make any money on it, or put that money to work for you? That's all I'm asking you to do.

And you don't have to do this alone. Excellent help is available. You're not going to say, "Go buy me ten shares of whatever company you hit with a dart." If you're just starting, without a good deal of money, you'll be using a mutual fund. The fund managers will pick the stocks for you. All you have to pick is a well-known family of funds, such as Vanguard or Fidelity (see the list on page 137), and they'll provide you with literature that will explain how simple investing is. They'll also provide benchmarks to help you judge how well the funds have done through the years, and you'll take comfort from that record. Just as you've proven yourself a good mother, or a good assistant, or a good wife over the long haul, the managers of these funds know that their ability will be judged by their performance—in concrete numbers—over a period of years.

I don't know where to start. I have no goals.

Not knowing where you're going means that you're the ideal person for the exercises in this book. More than anyone else, you need to start working on your finances. I don't care if you're 21 or 70: Don't be embarrassed that this is your first step. Better to take that step now than never to take it at all.

Fill out all the forms. Do all the exercises. Your goal: to see what you need and what you can save. How do you want to live later in life? Where do you want to be in twenty years? Once you can answer those questions, you can make your plan a possibility. Then grow into it.

Begin by thinking about where you want to be in the future, then work backwards. If you want to be retired, calculate how much money you'll need then, and see if you have any way of getting there. Do you want to change careers? See whether you have enough money put away to support that decision. Are you ready to start investing your money? Make sure that you don't have any credit-card debt before you start putting your money into investments that probably won't earn as much as you're paying in interest on that debt.

Can I take care of everything at the only place where I feel comfortable—my local bank?

Once upon a time the answer to this question was no. But things are changing. Banks are now selling mutual funds, for instance. They also sell individual stocks. But you probably want more than a bank can offer: real estate, bonds, investment advice, long-term planning, and so on. So try to go past banks, and investigate other possibilities.

I'm scared of investing. Can't you lose money that way?

Sure. If you invest poorly, you'll do poorly. If you invest for the short term without knowing what you're doing, you'll probably lose money. If you play around with vehicles you know nothing about, such as puts and calls, you'll lose money. But if you invest intelligently, the odds are that you'll do as well as anyone else.

Of course, if you invest in very safe vehicles, like CDs, you're insured up to $100,000, or if you invest in T-bills, you have nothing to worry about. But you won't make much money, either. You pay for that kind of insurance. Sleeping well at night isn't cheap. For most women, CDs and T-bills don't provide enough of a return. It's like treading water instead of swimming. You may stay afloat, but everyone else who's investing in funds that may pay up to 10 percent or more is swimming toward the coast, while you're just paddling in little circles.

But I'm still scared. How can I push myself?

I can understand. I, too, was terrified of losing my money. The way I got past my fear was that my fear was realized: I did lose my financial security. I did exactly the opposite of what I'm telling you to do now. I invested what I had left of my money and did everything wrong. But first of all, I didn't die when that happened. I endured the loss of the money. And also, I learned a lesson. So the next time

I went out to invest, I did things right, and got my money back in spades—and a career to boot.

My problem back then was that I picked a stockbroker who was more interested in having fun gambling with my money than in making smart choices. Investing is not the same as playing craps in Vegas. Just because an investment moves up and down doesn't mean that investing is a game. Life has its up and downs, too. Today you're happy, and you love your husband, tomorrow you hate him. Do you leave him? Of course not. You don't act on impulse. You act intelligently. And it's the same with money. Act intelligently, and you'll get intelligent results.

I still don't even want to start.

I don't blame you. But you do have to. And I know that can be scary.

Try to think about it in terms of driving a car. When you first sit behind the wheel, you're scared. The car is this great big thing that seems uncontrollable, and yet everyone else seems to handle it. But you can't. Then you try, and lo and behold, it isn't as hard as it seems. Investing is much the same. Yes, it looks scary at first. And yes, after a while, it isn't scary. Repeat after me: There's nothing to be afraid of.

Let's talk about fear. Fear has been a human trait ever since there have been humans. Fear can be good: It keeps us from playing with things we shouldn't play with. You should be afraid of fire, for example, and of taking stupid risks. Then there are things you fear because they represent the unknown. And sometimes the unknown is scary only because it's just that: unknown, unfamiliar, strange. A dark room can be frightening—until you turn on the lights and are comforted as you discover you're in your kitchen or bedroom. Well, to many women investing can seem like a dark room—mostly because women have been kept away from it for so many generations—but once you get inside and turn on the lights of knowledge, you see there's nothing to be afraid of.

So try to figure out why you're afraid of something you don't need to fear. In my case, it was because my father said I wasn't good in math and my mother told me it wasn't feminine to deal with money. Also, I was afraid to make mistakes and look like a fool. Examine your own reasons, and then try to get over your hesitation. Otherwise you may end up looking foolish only because everyone else out there is making money, and you're not. Now that's a good reason to feel silly.

Let's say I pick a money manager to help me. How do I know if he or she is any good?

First, bear in mind that you don't have to look for the top performer. That's not necessarily a badge of honor. People with stellar results one year often have bad results the next. All you want is someone who's honest, who works with integrity, who helps you understand what you're doing, and who keeps your portfolio performing at a level comparable to other people's. If your portfolio is down 10 percent when everyone else's is up 20 percent, there's something wrong. But if your manager is in the middle somewhere, that means you're getting a steady, reliable performance without a lot of volatility.

How do you find this person? If she's good, she'll have a reputation. Ask all your friends for names. Look in the papers and in magazines. And when you meet her, ask for references, just as you would with a doctor.

A few other things: Find out if she is abreast of the newest investment vehicles. Does she keep up with her education? Is she a stable person? You don't want some wacko managing your money. Is she keeping your investments within your own risk parameters? Is she helping *you* set parameters? And, can you talk to her? Does she listen? Do you like her? Remember, you want this to be a long-term relationship.

Are there any basic rules to keep in mind for investing?

The most important thing is to set your asset allocation first. See the risk questionnaire on page 123. You need to know yourself: Are you aggressive? Are you conservative? Are you awake every night worrying about individual stocks? Do you think the world is coming to an end? Do you hide money under your mattress? Do you think you can do no wrong? Once you know your psychological attitudes, you can figure out your financial profile.

What if another stock market crash is on the way?

When you start asking questions like that, you know you're conservative.

Anyway, part of what caused the crash was the rules. At that time, you could buy on margin, meaning you could borrow up to 75 percent of what you were buying. So when the market plummeted, people couldn't pay their debts.

A smart manager won't let you do things like that. Don't spend what you don't have. For now, be conservative: Pay for your stock.

The market has the equivalent of emotional states. They come and they go; they perform badly and then they bounce back. If you have a bad mood, you don't act on it (I hope). If you don't like your husband today, you probably won't divorce him, because you know that feeling will pass. The same is true of a stock. Just because it had one or two bad days, you shouldn't sell it.

Why do I have to care about something as morbid as estate planning?

For your family's sake. Because if you don't, when you're gone, your relatives may fight over your money in such horrible ways that you'll be glad you're dead. Do you really want to see Auntie Em divorce Uncle Ed over your emerald brooch? Just as you need to take care of your finances while you're alive, you need to determine what will become of them when you're gone. It doesn't matter how old you are, or how many assets you have. Do it. Do it now.

What are my assets?

Your real estate, stocks, bonds, mutual-fund shares, and cash, as well as any tangible personal property, such as furniture, cars, or jewelry; business or partnership interests; jointly owned property in any of the above categories; life insurance; and retirement plans.

The laws vary concerning joint ownership with a spouse and/or with others, although generally if you jointly own property with a spouse, one-half of the property's value is included as an asset of the estate. If you jointly own property with another (unrelated) person, 100 percent of the property will be included in your estate, unless you can prove that the joint owner contributed some or all of the consideration for the property.

I've heard that if it is worth less than a certain amount of money,
an estate won't be taxed. But I keep hearing different figures.
Which is correct?

The number you hear keeps changing for a good reason: That's the new law. It used to be that an estate with assets of less than $600,000 was not federally taxable. However, in the tax-reform bill that passed in 1997, that amount changed. Typically, the lawmakers did not simply change the figure. Under the new system, the cutoff point will increase in varying increments for ten years until it hits $1,000,000. In 1998 the figure was $625,000. In 1999 it'll be $650,000. And so on until 2006.

By the way, if you have an estate worth $800,000, the government won't simply deduct $650,000 and tax the rest. They'll tax the entire $800,000, and *then* subtract $650,000 worth of credits. Otherwise, it would be too easy to figure out the tax. And the powers that be never seem to want that to happen.

Are there exceptions to that cutoff?

Of course. It wouldn't be a federal law if it didn't have exceptions. If you leave all your money to your spouse, then the spouse won't have to pay any taxes on it, no matter how much you have. Although (of course) there are exceptions to this rule, too. Ask your estate planner for advice.

What's the best way to avoid estate taxes?

Give, give, and give. Isn't it nice that the government wants you to be generous? Who knew? But you can give away $10,000 a year to anyone you want, and never have to worry about it being taxed. That means a married couple can give someone $20,000 each year without any tax consequences.

You can also pay someone's educational or medical bills, and not have to worry about being taxed on that gift, either.

Taxes confuse me. Can you tell me the single most important thing to
keep in mind?

Most people are confused by taxes. And they should be. Sometimes it seems the government has gone out of its way to make it impossible for any normal person to understand the present tax code. But there is one thing to keep in mind, something that, in the long run, could make all the difference. *Be honest.* Sound simple? It is. Just do it. Sure, there's always a temptation to hide income. And maybe you'll get away with it. But maybe you won't. Do you want to risk going to jail just to have the money to buy an extra TV set? You won't be able to watch your own TV in your jail cell anyway.

Live by the rules. (And be careful to note that they change. In 1998 Congress rewrote some of them. It will happen again.)

What if I don't want to do my own taxes?

Half the country agrees with you. They hire someone else. So you can, too. Just make sure she's able and honest. Don't look for one who winks at you and hints that she can save you more money than you ever thought possible. Find one who plays by the rules.

Taxes I can handle, but insurance puts me to sleep. What should I do?

Get a great agent. Just as with taxes, the person you work with says it all. Find someone intelligent and capable. Then your insurance needs will be covered intelligently and capably.

Do I really need insurance?

Do you need to breathe? Yes. Insurance is what keeps you from going bankrupt should your life's circumstances go awry. All you need is for one person to slip and fall on your pavement, and boom! There goes your life's savings to pay for his broken ankle, as well as his psychological suffering.

What are the major types of insurance?

As mentioned on page 118, you may need life insurance to replace your wage income in the event of your death, as well as for estate taxes if you have assets, and possibly for investment purposes.

You need automobile insurance to cover your own liability if you hurt someone else, to cover your own medical and automobile costs if you are injured or your car is damaged, and for financial protection against an incident involving someone who's uninsured.

You need disability insurance to replace as much of your income as possible in case of a long-term disability.

You need homeowner's insurance to insure your property against theft or destruction. If you rent, renter's insurance protects your personal property similarly.

You need personal liability insurance to protect your personal assets from a personal liability lawsuit.

You need professional liability insurance to protect your professional assets from a job-related lawsuit.

Do I really need all those?

Life insurance isn't necessary for everyone—if you're a single person without dependents, your money would be better spent elsewhere. And if you're married, your husband's policy may well be all you need.

But the others? In most circumstances, yes, you need them.

There are also a few other important types of insurance, such as long-term care insurance, which helps you look after yourself in the event of a prolonged illness or disability. We often think that Medicare will cover all our nursing home expenses, but that's not the case.

Unfortunately, long-term care insurance can be very expensive. But the younger you are, the cheaper it is, so if you can afford it, it's good to buy it now.

Speaking of growing old, can't I count on social security to take care of me?

When last I calculated, I'm going to be getting about $1,300 a month when I turn 65. Needless to say, that's not enough. And who knows—that's what I get only if social security is still around. Estimates vary as to how long it will remain solvent, but the betting is that we're not talking about forever.

And even if it doesn't run out, or if the government finds a way to reform it, social security isn't a full retirement program. When the system was designed, social security paid small but reasonable benefits. Inflation has taken care of that over the years.

There's a real likelihood that social security *won't* be around. So the answer is: No, you can't count on it.

What should I do then?

Haven't you been listening? Save!

I'm not 65 yet. I'm not even 35. Do I really need to worry about my financial future? Anything can happen in the next thirty years.

You mean, a man can happen? Maybe he will, maybe he won't. You can't depend on someone else to secure your financial future. The world has changed. Anyway, the best time to start thinking about your retirement is when you're young, so you can put the magic of compounding to work for you over the years.

What else besides investments takes the place of social security?

All the other retirement savings plans you've heard about: 401(k), 403(b), pensions, IRAs (Individual Retirement Accounts), Keoghs, SEPs (Simplified Employee Pensions), pension plans, etc. All of these plans offer you ways to grow your money tax-free. Tax-free! Any time the government offers you a way to make money without taxation, jump on it. Such chances are unlikely to come around often.

A **401(k)** is a plan that allows you to put aside a portion of your pre-tax salary and place it into a retirement account where it will grow tax-free. Thus your overall taxable income is reduced by the amount you contribute, plus you get the tax-free savings. On top of that, many employers match your contributions. You may invest this money as you see fit, but with some exceptions: You can't withdraw money without penalties before you reach age 59½. You can loan yourself part of the money whenever you wish, however. There are other rules and considerations to keep in mind, so study your plan well.

A **403(b)** is for those who work for charitable or other not-for-profit organizations. It's similar to a 401(k), but contains enough differences to require some careful analysis if you qualify for one.

If you're self-employed, or employed but not part of a company retirement plan (or if your yearly income is below a certain level), you can set aside money for retirement using pre-tax dollars through a tax-deductible **IRA** account. This means that if you make $50,000 a year, and put aside $2,000 (the maximum contribution for a single person), and had no other deductions, you'd be taxed on only $48,000 of your income. Even if you're employed and don't qualify for tax-deductible contributions, you can still put aside the money in an IRA and earn tax-free interest. Funds in an IRA can't be withdrawn until you reach age 59½ without resulting in a 10 percent penalty, and will be taxed at your normal tax rate.

A **Keogh** is a retirement plan that anyone with income from self-employment can set up. As with an IRA, the earnings on your savings aren't taxable, and the contribution is also tax-deductible. Also as in other plans, you can't touch it until you're 59½ without penalties. There are several kinds of Keoghs, but all allow you to put aside more per year than you could in an IRA. There are also careful formulas telling you what portion of your income can be contributed, so once again, study the plan carefully before taking action.

A **Simplified Employee Pension plan** (SEP) is also tailor-made for anyone who has some self-employment income. A SEP is deposited directly into your IRA accounts, and again, specific formulas direct how much you can contribute, and when.

Pension plans, the most traditional form of corporate retirement plans, vary widely from company to company, but there are two basic types: defined-benefit plans, in which the amount you receive when you retire is determined in advance, and defined-contribution plans, in which you don't know how much you'll have to retire on until you actually retire. You should check with your employer to see which type, if either, you have, and save according to the rules. Pension plans work best for those who stay put at one company, since most plans require that you work a certain number of years before you're vested—meaning that you are a part of the plan.

Roth Individual Retirement Account (IRA): Unlike the traditional IRA, this brand new IRA is nondeductible when you make contributions (the traditional IRA is tax-deductible). However, there are no taxes on withdrawals after you retire and begin using the money in it. Of course, you'll need to check out the enormous number of government rules and regulations governing the Roth, but there are some terrific advantages to the new system particularly if you're young. (Roth, by the way, is the senator from Delaware responsible for all this.)

GLOSSARY

Below are definitions of some of the many words and phrases you'll be hearing as you start paying more attention to your money. You certainly don't have to know what all these terms mean right away, but keep this glossary handy so that you can look them up when necessary. It's like speaking a foreign language: At first it all seems somewhat overwhelming, but once you get the hang of it, you may be surprised at how frequently you use these terms yourself.

annuity: A contract guaranteeing a fixed income for either a specified amount of time or for life. The advantage is guaranteed income; the disadvantage is a low rate of return. In some states you can buy them at banks, but for the most part they come to you via your favorite insurance company.

asset allocation: A fancy term for a method to keep your eggs from staying in one basket, i.e., distributing your money among many different investments, such as stocks, bonds, and real estate.

asset management account: An account through which you let someone (me, for instance) take care of your assets and grow them yearly. Normally, asset managers work with portfolios worth more than $200,000, but there are no hard and fast rules. The amount you're charged generally depends on how much money you have, and it's usually figured as a percentage of total assets.

bear market: When the bears (the sleepy people who don't have faith in the economy) take over and the stock market falls.

bearer bond: A bond whose ownership is not recorded, but is payable to anyone who physically owns it.

big board: This refers specifically to the actual electronic board at the New York Stock Exchange that reports the stocks' ups and downs during the day. It also can mean the stock exchange itself.

bull market: When the bulls (the people charging forward with good news about the economy) are leading the way, and the stock market rises.

blue-chip stock: A common stock issued by a well-known, highly reputable company with a history of making money and paying dividends. These stocks are usually not big risks, and as a result, they are not known to earn a spectacular return (the name derives from the blue chips in poker, which are the most valuable, and the ones my father the gambler lost the most). A blue-chip bond also means one that is safe and solid rather than risky.

bond: Unlike common stock, where your money buys you a share of ownership in a company, a bond is an investment vehicle in the form of a debt owed to you. You are paid back for your loan with interest at a rate extending over the period of the bond. Bonds are issued not only by private corporations, but also by federal, state, and local governments.

book value per share: The worth of each share of stock; it is derived by dividing the number of outstanding shares by total stockholder equity. For example, if a company's total stockholder equity is $100,000,000, and there are 50 million shares outstanding, by dividing the first sum by the second, you get a book value per share of $2.

bubble: What happens when an investment vehicle becomes inflated beyond its value. When the bubble "bursts," the price drops.

capital gain: An increase in the market value of an asset above the price you originally paid for it. You don't have to worry about the tax consequences until you sell the asset.

capital loss: The opposite of capital gain. In this case, the market value of your asset has decreased since you bought it.

cashier's check: A check that a financial institution draws on itself in exchange for money you pay directly to it. Like a certified check, it's a guaranteed form of payment, so companies such as movers are likely to ask for one of these rather than a personal check, which may bounce (while you've moved to another state).

certified check: A personal check that your bank guarantees to pay; the money is deducted from your account before the person to whom it's made out cashes it.

certificates of deposit (CD): Remember going to the bank for the first time as a child to open up your $5 account? A CD is the adult version of that: Here, with a minimum deposit and a specified period of time in mind (anywhere from a month to eight years), you can place a sum of money in the bank and get a slightly better interest rate than if you simply put it into your savings account. CD's are insured by the government up to $100,000.

chapter 7, 11, and 13: Court-approved plans for declaring bankruptcy.

closed-end (mutual) fund: A mutual fund with a limited number of shares that are traded in markets much as stocks are traded. Unlike most mutual funds, where you can buy in whenever you want, here you can only buy in when someone is willing to sell shares to you. The opposite is an open-end fund, which will always accept you and your money.

commission: The fee you pay to a broker or any other agent for negotiating a sale.

common stock: An ownership share in a publicly or privately held company. Common stock is what we usually mean when we talk about owning stock. In return for investing your money in your chosen company, you get to share in the wealth if the company, and therefore the stock, sees an increase in value; in addition, you can receive dividends and get to vote for the firm's directors.

compound interest: The interest that accumulates when earnings over a specific period of time are added to the principal, so that the interest for the next period includes the principal **and** the accumulated interest.

convertible bond: A bond (or a form of debt, remember?) that can be exchanged for common stock (or another security) instead of getting your cash back, as is usually the case.

coupon bond: Another term for bearer bond.

deflation: A time when prices decrease, or, when the value of money increases.

discount broker: Someone who charges low fees to buy or sell your stocks; usually you can expect to get no advice or research along the way, which is why regular brokers feel they can charge you more.

dividend: A share of the company's net income distributed to its stockholders. This can be paid in money or in stocks.

Dow Jones Industrial Average: For years I used to wonder, who is this Dow Jones guy? (After all, my brother once had a friend named Jim Beam.) All day on the radio I would hear Dow Jones this, Dow Jones that. Actually Dow Jones is an index representing the composite average of the thirty most influential large stocks on the New York Stock Exchange, reported each day the market is in session.

There are many other indexes, too:

There's one for the entire New York Stock Exchange, and there's one for every economic sector, such as industrial stocks; there's one for every other market, too, including the American Stock Exchange, European and Asian markets, bonds, over-the-counter stocks, and many more.

durable power of attorney: A document that allows you to appoint another person to make decisions on your behalf.

earnings per share (EPS): A corporation's net income divided by the total number of outstanding shares. Many analysts consider EPS the most important indicator of a company's strength.

equity investments: When someone's being fancy, they may refer to stocks as equity, or equity instruments. I myself, prefer to use the word "stock" so that people know what I'm talking about.

Federal Reserve System (the Fed): Our country's central monetary authority. The Fed's board of governors oversees twelve Federal Reserve Banks, located across America, that deal with banks rather than the public.

fixed-income instruments: Another, fancier term for a bond (see above).

futures market: A place where commodities or securities are bought and sold at prices fixed at the moment for delivery at a specified future date. These self-regulating markets include the Amex Commodity Exchange, the Commodity Exchange, Inc. (COMEX), the New York Mercantile Exchange, the Chicago Board of Trade, the Kansas City Board of Trade, the New York Coffee, Sugar and Cocoa Exchange, and many more across the country.

401(k): A plan that allows you to set aside a portion of your pretax salary and place it into a retirement account where it will grow tax-free. Your overall taxable income is reduced by the amount you contribute, plus you get the tax-free savings. On top of that, many employers match your contributions. You may invest this money as you see fit, but with some exceptions, you can't withdraw money without penalties before you reach age 59½. You can loan yourself part of the money whenever you wish, however. There are other rules and considerations to keep in mind, so study your plan well. (A 403(b) is for those who work for not-for-profit organizations. It's similar to a 401(k), but contains enough differences to require some careful analysis if you qualify for one.)

glamour stock: As its name implies, a stock that investors seem to really like a lot, for instance, Internet stocks such as America Online or Amazon.com. These stocks are often volatile, which means you have to have a strong stomach to tolerate swings in their performance.

growth stock: A stock that has exhibited faster-than-average gains in earnings over the last few years and is expected to continue to show high levels of profit growth. These stocks are usually riskier investments than blue-chip stocks.

inflation: When prices increase, as opposed to deflation.

interest: The amount of money charged to a borrower by a lender.

junk bond: These are high-yield bonds that are considered more speculative. Again, they can pay a lot, but you have to risk more. Junk bonds have ratings below investment grade (at or below Ba1 on Moody's, at or below BB+ on Standard & Poor's), or are unrated.

Keogh: A type of retirement plan that any-one with income from self-employment income can set up. As with an IRA, the earnings on your savings aren't taxable, and the contribution is also tax-deductible. Also as in other retirement plans, you can't touch it until you're 59½. There are several kinds of Keoghs, but all allow you to contribute more each year than an IRA. There are also complex formulas telling you what portion of your income can be contributed, so once again, study the plan carefully before taking action.

large capitalization stocks: Stocks of companies calculated to be worth over one billion dollars (referred to as "large cap" stocks).

last-survivor insurance: A type of life insurance that insures two or more people and pays a death benefit at the time of the last death. Last-survivor insurance is used most frequently to insure the lives of a married couple. The advantage of last-survivor insurance is that estate taxes aren't paid until the second death. When a spouse dies, the surviving spouse doesn't pay taxes. But when the second spouse dies, estate taxes (for the wealthy) can take more than half of a family's inheritance.

life-insurance premium: The amount of money you agree to pay for life insurance. If you have fixed premiums, then you must pay your premiums every year for as long as the policy states. If you have flexible premiums, you pay them as often as you wish, in whatever amount you wish, subject to maximum and minimum amounts. Indeterminate premiums are premiums which can be adjusted by the insurance company, either up or down.

liquidity: If your money is liquid, it's obtainable quickly. For example, if your money is in a checking account, you can just write a check to withdraw it. That's liquidity.

living will: A document that allows you to make decisions about your medical treatment before a serious or terminal illness arises. See the form on page 167.

margin: A form of loan: a percentage of money deposited with a broker as a provision against loss on transactions. For example, borrowing 50 cents to purchase a dollar's worth of stock. During the 1987 stock market crash, some people had to sell their stocks because they had used margin you are allowed by law to borrow. When the market goes down dramatically, the margin requires buyers to put up even more money on what they owe, and if they can't, they have to sell stock.

market risk: The risk incurred due to the stock market's frequent ups and downs. The day after you've invested in a stock or bond, the price will most likely change for the better or worse, even if it's just by a fraction. Except for cash equivalents, all investments share some degree of change, or volatility.

marketability: If your investment is marketable, it means you can resell it for cash.

maturity: A state we all aspire to, and the date when the principal amount on a bond is repaid.

Medicaid: A public-assistance program, through both federal and state governments, that helps pay for the medical costs of the poor or disabled.

Medicare: The federal government program that gives senior citizens over the age of 65 (or, with special qualifying circumstances, under 65) major insurance coverage. Yes, it's free, but that doesn't mean that you shouldn't consider other options, such as long-term care insurance.

municipal bond: A bond issued by a local government, or a not-for-profit institution. The interest is exempt from federal income tax and, in the state of issue, from state (and usually local) tax as well. Also called munies (not pronounced "Moonies").

mutual fund: A pool of financial assets in which individual investors buy shares in stocks, bonds, government securities, etc. The funds are managed by professionals, so investors can enjoy expert advice without having to go through a broker.

no-load fund: A mutual fund that sells its shares without your having to pay a commission.

over-the-counter stock: A stock (or an unlisted security) which is not sold on an organized stock exchange, usually because it's too small. NASDAQ (the National Association of Security Dealers Automated Quotation System) is an entire network of these stocks.

penny stock: A stock that is usually traded for less than a dollar a share (although rarely an actual penny). These stocks are often highly speculative and it takes real knowledge to make any money on them, even if you buy them cheaply.

pension plan: The most traditional form of corporate retirement plans. These plans vary widely from company to company, but there are two basic types: defined-benefit plans, in which the amount you receive when you retire is determined in advance, and defined-contribution plans, in which you don't know how much you'll have to retire on until you actually retire. You should check with your employer to see which plan, if either, you have, and save according to the rules. Pension plans work best for those who stay put at one company, since most plans require that you work a certain number of years before you're vested—meaning that you have become a part of the plan.

preferred stock: An ownership share in a company differing from common stock in that you are usually paid fixed dividends.

price-to-earnings ratio: The ratio of a stock's price to its earnings per share. This figure is calculated by dividing the per-share earnings of the company into the current selling price of the stock. This formula can tell you the number of times its earnings for which a stock sells.

principal: The original amount of money lent, not including profits and interest; or, the amount of money put at risk in an investment.

prime rate: The interest rate that banks charge corporations.

probate: The court proceedings that occur after someone dies to determine the validity of his or her will. The process considers the distribution of assets left behind in his or her name (and, if the estate is large enough, which assets are to be taxed).

proxy: A person authorized to act for another. If you want to vote at your stock-holder's meeting, but you can't make it, you can authorize someone to vote for you; that person is your proxy. The word also refers to the written authorization itself.

Roth Individual Retirement Account (IRA): Unlike with a traditional IRA, the contributions to this IRA are nondeductible (traditional IRA contributions are tax-deductible). But there are no taxes on the withdrawals when you retire. Of course, you'll need to check out the enormous number of government rules and regulations involved, but

there are some terrific advantages to this new system particularly if you're young.

Securities and Exchange Commission: The U.S. agency responsible for regulating and supervising the securities markets. The SEC was established in the early 1930s after the great stock market crash.

SEP: A Simplified Employee Pension. This type of retirement plan is tailor-made for anyone who has some self-employment income; it is deposited directly into your IRA account. As with a standard IRA, there are restrictions on when you can withdraw money (and how much).

small-capitalization stocks: Stocks of companies valued at under $250 million (referred to as "small cap" stocks).

speculative stock: Any stock—usually one with a great deal of volatility—on which you're willing to take a risk in order to make a good deal of money.

stock: Officially, shares of capital in a publicly traded company.

term insurance: A kind of insurance policy that pays money, or a death benefit, if death occurs before a certain date. This date is called the term of the policy. The premiums you pay usually don't increase for the duration of the policy, and you may be able to renew it at the end of the term.

Treasury bills: Fixed-income instruments (bonds) issued with maturities of three months, six months, or one year (although this may change). Since they are guaranteed by the government, they are very safe (but not very profitable).

triple tax-exempt: When you own a fund

that's triple tax-exempt, it means your earnings are exempt from federal, state, and local taxes. (If you see the term "double exempt," it means exempt from federal and state taxes only.)

universal life insurance: A type of life insurance that provides lots of flexibility. First appearing in the 1970s, these policies allow you to change the death benefit whenever you wish, and you can pay premiums as often or as infrequently as you wish, and in any amount you wish, subject to limitations. This insurance works like a bank account into which your premiums are added, and interest is credited by the insurance company (with certain charges deducted). Your account has a guaranteed interest rate, and if the insurance company is earning enough on the investments it makes with your money to pay you more, it usually will. Guaranteed charges are always shown on your policy, but companies frequently charge less than these guaranteed rates. You may also run into a "surrender charge," which reduces the amount you can withdraw from your policy. The surrender charge decreases over time, and usually lapses entirely fifteen or twenty years after you've bought the policy.

variable life insurance: This type of policy resembles universal life insurance (see above) except that, instead of the insurance company holding your money and investing it for you, you can invest it in a variable account yourself. Variable accounts are structured like mutual funds, and are often managed by mutual-fund companies. The cash value of your investment will rise and fall with the account you choose. As in a mutual fund, your money can grow quickly in one

of these accounts. But you risk losses if the value of your funds falls. Since you'll usually have a choice of several funds, and you can even choose to divide your money among these funds, you get more control over how your money is invested than you do with universal life or whole-life insurance.

volatility: Not unlike my own moods, this term refers to the ups and downs of certain stocks that are sensitive to outside news and conditions.

W-2 form: The information sent to you by your employer documenting your wages, along with the amounts withheld for federal and state income tax, and social security tax.

whole-life insurance: The most common kind of life insurance. It comes in many forms, and its death benefit is payable when you die (or, if you're lucky enough to live past 100, which the insurance company seems to equate with death).

The premiums for whole-life insurance can be either fixed or indeterminate, and you can pay them for as long as you live, or to a certain age or for a certain number of years. In the latter case the policy is called a limited-payment policy, and its premiums are generally larger than those for a policy in which the premiums are paid for life.

yield: The income earned on an investment (usually expressed as a percentage of the amount paid).

zero-coupon bond: A bond bought at a deep discount. It pays no interest until it matures, at which time the holder gets the bond's face value plus all the interest accrued over the years.

Different Types of Mutual Funds

aggressive funds: As their name implies, funds that are set up to give you maximum growth, with risk, i.e., investing in speculative stocks. These aren't designed to give you present income, or make you sleep well at night. But if you stay put over twenty years, you may sleep very well indeed.

balanced funds: Funds with the goal of trying to conserve your principal, pay you income, and grow reasonably over the years. Here you'll find your money in solid stocks and bonds.

bond funds: Funds that invest in bonds from companies and the government. They will provide you with income, but the amount you're paid, and the risk you take, depends which bonds are in the fund. They can be risky, which means they may pay well or they may default; or they can be conservative, meaning they'll provide steady income without much chance for big profits.

equity funds: Funds that invest in shares of companies.

foreign funds: Funds investing in companies outside the United States. The largest holdings are usually in European or Japanese corporations.

Ginnie Mae funds: Funds that invest in mortgage securities backed by the Government National Mortgage Association (GNMA). Ginnie Maes are guaranteed by the U.S. Government and therefore aren't likely (we hope) to fail.

global equity funds: Funds similar to equity funds, but composed of international securities rather than domestic ones.

growth funds: Funds investing in steadily performing stocks that are considered likely to outperform the general market. These funds are best for long-term investments.

growth-and-income funds: Funds offering an investment compromise: Here you get some dividend income and some long-term growth. For those who want a little of everything.

index funds: Funds based on an index, usually the Standard & Poor's index, meaning that your money invested in such a fund goes up (or down) exactly as the S&P stocks do. Although they might seem to be brainless, index funds very often beat the performance of carefully managed funds.

money-market funds: Funds that invest in short-term securities, such as certificates of deposit or government securities. They tend to be very safe, not offering you a great chance to make a lot of money. On the other hand, these are great sleep-at-night offerings.

natural resources and precious metal funds: As the name implies, these funds invest in specific companies working in specific areas such as diamond mining.

sector funds: Funds that invest in specialized areas. Remember in the film *The Graduate,* when the key word was "plastics"? These funds try to pinpoint today's hot industry and invest in that particular field, or sector, be it oil, or technology, or health care.

tax-exempt funds: Funds that invest in government or other tax-free bonds, so that your earnings are tax-exempt.

APPENDIX A: LIVING WILL

I, _____, being of sound mind, make this statement as a directive to be followed if I become permanently unable to participate in decisions regarding my medical care. These instructions reflect my firm and settled commitment to decline medical treatment under the circumstances indicated below:

I direct my attending physician to withhold or withdraw treatment that merely prolongs my dying, if I should be in an *incurable or irreversible mental or physical condition with no reasonable expectation of recovery.*

These instructions apply if I am a) *in a terminal condition;* b) *permanently unconscious;* or c) *if I am minimally conscious but have irreversible brain damage and will never regain the ability to make decisions and express my wishes.*

I direct that treatment be limited to measures to keep me comfortable and to relieve pain, including any pain that might occur by withholding or withdrawing treatment.

While I understand that I am not legally required to be specific about future treatments, *if I am in the condition(s) described above I feel especially strongly about the following forms of treatment:*

I do not want cardiac resuscitation.
I do not want mechanical respiration.
I do not want tube feeding.
I do not want antibiotics.
I do want maximum pain relief.

These directions express my legal right to refuse treatment, under the law of the state of _____. I intend my instructions to be carried out, unless I have rescinded them in a new writing or by clearly indicating that I have changed my mind.

IN WITNESS WHEREOF, I have hereunto set my hand this _____ day of _____, _____.

_____

Witness: _____
Address: _____

Witness: _____
Address: _____

APPENDIX B: HEALTH-CARE PROXY

I, _____, hereby appoint my _____, _____,of [city,state], as my health-care agent to make any and all health-care decisions for me, except to the extent that I state otherwise. This proxy shall take effect when and if I become unable to make my own health-care decisions.

I direct my proxy to make health-care decisions in accord with my wishes and limitations as stated below, or as she otherwise knows. I declare that I have discussed with my agent my wishes regarding the following: artificial nutrition and hydration; artificial respiration; cardiopulmonary resuscitation; antipsychotic medication; electronconvulsive therapy; antibiotics; psychosurgery; dialysis; transplantation; blood transfusions; abortion; and sterilization, and it is my intention that my agent shall have full authority to withhold or withdraw these measures or procedures.

Unless I revoke it, this proxy shall remain in effect indefinitely. These directions express my legal right to have my proxy make health-care decisions on my behalf. I intend my instructions to be carried out, unless I have rescinded them in a new writing or by clearly indicating that I have changed my mind.

IN WITNESS WHEREOF, I have hereunto set my hand this _____ day of _____, _____.

_____

Statement by Witnesses:
I declare that the person who signed this document is personally known to me and appears to be of sound mind and acting of his-her own free will. He-she signed this document in our presence.

Witness: _____

Address: _____

Witness: _____

Address: _____

INDEX